MARINE ELECTRONICS HANDBOOK

MARINE ELECTRONICS HANDBOOK

Choice, Installation and Use

COLIN JONES

WATERLINE

First published in the UK in 1997
by Waterline Books, an imprint of Airlife Publishing Ltd

British Library Cataloguing-in-Publication Data
A catalogue record for this book
is available from the British Library

ISBN 1 85310 882 0

Typeset by Phoenix Typesetting, Ilkley, West Yorkshire.
Printed in England by St. Edmundsbury Press Ltd., Bury St Edmunds, Suffolk.

Waterline Books
an imprint of Airlife Publishing Ltd
101 Longden Road, Shrewsbury, SY3 9EB, England

Contents

Introduction

The *Marine Electronics Handbook* is offered as an anthology of facts, theory, our practical experience and fun. Its primary inspiration was the feedback from a series of articles written for *Practical Boat Owner* and *Yachting Monthly*, for the leisure side, and a regular page in *Fishing News Weekly*, which serves the professional trawlermen.

Much of this material was collected and collated during the annual six months when we work and play with our office and home on a Colvic Watson motor sailer, which has taken us to many fascinating places and whose electronics have guided us to places we might not otherwise have seen and helped us through adventures which would have been impossible without them.

We have also learned a lot – and gathered not a few scallops along the way – by setting up our 5.8-metre dive RIB and researching topics for *Diver Magazine* and *Boat Mart*, whose readers have frequently sought our help while they try to find a way out of the marine electronics maze.

The third inspiration continues to be those quayside chats with other RIB drivers and the long pleasant hours spent with other yacht owners in the cockpits of our respective boats. Inevitably, the conversation touches on anything which makes life at sea easier, safer and more enjoyable. Boat electrics and electronics are often part of the conversational bill of fare.

All these sources seem to share a combination of curiosity and anxiety about what is certainly the fastest moving department of boating life and business. These friends and correspondents confess to being confused.

'What should I buy?' is probably our most frequently received plea for guidance. Marine equipment is expensive, so there is an understandable anxiety that a combination of poor advice from salesmen and insufficient knowledge of a complex subject will result in disappointment and even in the financial waste of buying the wrong tool. This is always tinged with the fear that what you buy for use this season, might be out of date and have less back-up next year.

Knowledge is power – which is where we come in with the hope that what follows will give you enough knowledge of equipment fundamentals to cut a swathe of clarity through sales spiels and brochure obfuscation. In the chapters which follow, we have done this for as many electronics departments as possible and hope to have created an enjoyable and informative read. There is certainly much to tell you about.

Knowledge is power and power is safety.

Our own boat is obviously well equipped, so we have twenty-five separate units telling us things which we deem to be important. They are:

battery charge warning light
circuit monitor
oil pressure meter
voltmeter
ammeter
engine hour meter
engine temperature forward
engine temperature aft
tachometer
autopilot screen
chart plotter
main GPS
back-up GPS
inclinometer
compass
video fish finder
log
depth
wind
radar
VHF
barometer
Navtex
SSB radio
weatherfax.

When we recite this catalogue to visitors, they throw up their hands in contemplative horror at the amount of electrical current we must require. It is not generally appreciated just how little juice is needed for many of the tools above – mostly milliamps.

For test purposes, here in the office, I have a 10-amp-hour rechargeable battery intended to back up a burglar alarm. It will run a Global Positioning System (GPS) receiver for a week. Coupled to a 5-watt solar panel, it has not needed any other form of charge all winter.

On the boat, it is not the mainstream electronics which are the voltage gobblers but the fridge and the steaming lights which are the biggest culprits. We fitted enormous, overkill batteries to cope with these.

The other frequent questions are 'Do you really need all this equipment' and 'Don't they take some of the satisfaction out of navigation and boat pilotage?' The answer to both parts is 'no'.

We could manage the boat with less gear, but returning to our *leitmotiv* of knowledge is power is safety, the skipper cannot have too much information to hand. A good seaman will use absolutely everything he can lay his hands on to make voyaging easier and safer – everything from sextant to boat computer.

If it makes the boat better and I can afford it, I should be stupid not to have it and to use it.

Electronic navigation is very satisfying in its own right. Done properly, there is no danger that it can replace traditional navigation skills. In fact it adds something to them. A second recurring theme on the following pages is just how comforting it can be when conditions are dark and difficult, but everything checks out against everything else. When you have done the plot and kept it up to date on a paper chart and your figures agree with what you programmed into the GPS and chart plotter and the radar distance and bearing also confirms the accuracy, that is a relief and a satisfaction. It creates a good feeling.

That could be our third recurring theme. If you are a newcomer to the fun and security of marine electronics, we hope you will be guided into our themes. If you are an electronics expert, we hope that you will enjoy sharing some of our diving and cruising experiences.

Chapter 1

The VHF Radio

In spite of all other electronic progress and the attractions of the new breed of electronic navigation aids, Very High Frequency (VHF) radio will always maintain its place towards the top of any boat owner's shopping list. We actually use our boat radio very infrequently, but I should feel very vulnerable if I ever went to sea without it. There is always the hope that you will never run into an on-board problem, but it is also a tremendous comfort to know that, *in extremis*, you can probably tell somebody where you are and be able to ask for help.

Because it is so universal and indispensable, the VHF radio is taken for granted even though most yachtsmen never lose that sense of mystique about how it works. There is frequent head scratching that on some days the signal seems to be almost unreadable over ten miles, yet I have frequently spoken to fellow radio amateurs in France, from the coast of Devon, using a handheld VHF rig. This is astonishing when you recall that radio waves are said to travel in a straight line, or line of sight, yet the Earth's curvature creates the equivalent of a 1,200-foot mountain between Devon and Brittany. Somehow the radio waves manage to get over it. This is a

real mystery because it does not always happen.

There is, nowadays, much less mystery about the actual black box, which is generally so reliable that we put it in the 'fit it and forget it' category. It seems that it has always been there and has always been the same. Yet, this most normal item of marine electronics is one of the least understood by most of its users and has also seen much surreptitious change since its early days. To get the most out of it, you really need to appreciate a little of how radio transmission (normally abbreviated to TX) and radio reception (briefly RX) work in the same unit, often called a transceiver and frequently written as TCVR.

Frequencies and Waves

Very briefly, it is the function of the TX circuitry to generate electromagnetic energy, which alternates between positive and negative cycles (sine wave) at a precisely known and variable number of sequences per second. This number of changes made per second is called the frequency. When you realise that the marine VHF calling and distress channel 16 operates at a frequency of 156.800 MegaHertz (MHz) or 156.8 million cycles per second, you see why it is called very high frequency. The next channel up the scale is Ch 17 and is only legally available to very low power units talking to each other on the same ship. This operates on 156.825 MHz.

Put another way, to go up one channel, you are only moving up 0.025 of a MHz from a base of 156,800,000 cycles per second. Such a small shift in such a short time span obviously requires some very sophisticated frequency-generating circuitry and equally high quality RX equipment. The mechanism must also be very stable so that one channel does not drift slightly and interfere with another.

How the electromagnetic energy gets from TX to RX is also worthy of comprehension. Again simplistically, when the sine wave is running from zero to its peak, the TX sends a positive voltage up the antenna. As it climbs it creates an alternating field of electrical and magnetic energy in the atmosphere outside the aerial.

As the wave goes negative and the sine curve descends to the base line and beyond, this field collapses – but not entirely. Some energy is left outside the antenna and is blasted away into 'the ether' by the next positive surge – and so on to create a series of pulses, or waves, travelling at the speed of light – 186,000 miles per second.

There are a number of other interesting facts about radio energy. It never really dies.

It attenuates into a weakness beyond the sensitivity of even present-day equipment, but even World War Two radio transmissions are still travelling somewhere out there in space.

To a radio wave, the molecules making up the structure of a wall are so wide apart that passing through is as easy as riding a bicycle through a set of football goal posts. If there are enough goal posts and they are not set up in parallel lines, that might slow you down and cause you to reduce power, but you would still get there. This explains why indoor aerials work, but do not work as well as their outside counterparts.

The Receiver

Logically, if there is all that radio frequency energy running around out there for infinite time (add in commercial radio, television, mobile phones, etc) then a simple aerial sticking up into the sky is going to be touched by all of them. How come they do not all emerge from the loudspeaker at the same time?

Luckily, most of them are so weak that they do not induce any voltage in the receiving antenna. Some energy waves (especially) of very high, or ultra high frequency, only travel in straight lines, so they are either totally blocked, or much impeded, by big

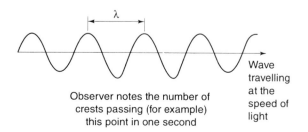

Observer notes the number of crests passing (for example) this point in one second

Wave travelling at the speed of light

1.1 Wavelength is peak-to-peak. Frequency is number of peaks per second

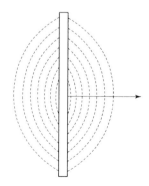

1.2 Electromagnetic field builds up outside the antenna and is blasted away by the next positive voltage surge.

buildings, mountains and the curvature of the Earth.

Of most importance is the fact that the RX circuitry is tuned only to receive incoming radio energy of a certain frequency. In the early days, this magic was performed by a small slice of quartz crystal cut so that it was only sensitive (and would only vibrate) at certain frequencies. Now, the control is electronic and is more precise, which reciprocally explains why the spacing between VHF channels can now be set at 25 KiloHertz (25 thousand cycles per second) rather than the old 50, which needed to be this wide because not all channels remained at precisely what they were nominally set at, so cross-channel interference was not unusual.

The All-important Antenna

These elementary principles go a long way to explain why serious radio practitioners are just as interested in the aerial as in the actual radio set.

Let us go back to the voltage/energy running up the antenna and then skating back down again at a precise number of cycles per second. For maximum efficiency, the descent should have reached the bottom before the next positive cycle starts its climb. If the aerial is of the wrong length, the voltage – say – will not have reached its nadir before the next lot starts to climb. There will be a clash between the upward and downward forces, resulting in signal distortion and loss of output power.

Most marine VHF aerials are 'cut' for the calling channel. Even though they operate well enough on something like Channel 80, whose frequency is far removed from the 156.800 MHz of Channel 16, an engineer with a meter would be able to detect a power drop.

This is often the answer to somebody grumbling that their radio does not seem to 'get out' on certain channels. They probably have an inferior antenna complaining that the TX frequency is not quite right for its length. It also explains the radio truism that

you can receive signals on a random length of wet string, but to transmit well your antenna needs to be professionally constructed to the correct length.

Here would be a good time to insert a word of warning. It is not good practice to take a Citizen Band mobile aerial, or an Amateur Radio bands 2-metre whip and expect to be able to use it on a marine rig. That could re-inject so much radio frequency (RF) energy back into the delicate transmission circuitry as to do serious damage.

Even worse is to neglect to connect up an antenna, but to depress the Push-to-talk button, generally on the microphone and used to generate the output energy. This means that the energy has nowhere to go except into its own internal wiring. A couple of seconds of such treatment can be bad and expensive news.

VHF Radio Range

'How far does your VHF radio go?' is probably the most frequent and the most naïve question ever asked. The questioner is under the common delusion that the possible distance between TX and RX points is decided by the superiority of one make of marine VHF radio over another. Broadly and narrowly speaking, this is just not true. A radio costing twice the price will not give you twice the distance.

The factors which decide VHF radio range are:

1. Output power.
2. Antenna efficiency.
3. Antenna altitude.
4. Atmospheric conditions.

These factors are listed in their approximate order of importance.

Output Power

Marine VHF radios are very strictly regulated and by international agreement. The maximum permitted output power is 25 watts. It is probable that even brand-new rigs never quite achieve this figure and almost certain that a radio which is a couple of years old and has never had a professional service will fall well short of it.

The fact that many older, unserviced rigs, generating less than the maximum wattage, still operate to their owners' satisfaction puts the importance of 'raw' power in its proper perspective. At ranges less than the maximum possible at the time, many TXs could be switched to the low power setting (usually 5 watts) without much perceivable drop in signal readability at the receiving end. When we are talking to marina offices and amongst a flotilla of cruising boats, switching to low power should be standard practice.

Antenna Efficiency

Antenna and aerial are technically synonymous and are the two most important words in radio of all kinds. If you have a £500 radio set and a £10 aerial, you have a set up which is worth no more than a tenner.

The importance of length has already been discussed, but a good antenna will also be constructed of the best materials, not only for good conductivity, but also for resistance to corrosion. The cable and plug joints must also be well made (to avoid power loss) and the feed from the back of the radio to the base of the aerial must be of entirely appropriate coaxial cable.

It is possible to construct a 'home brew' marine VHF aerial, but even though the author is a Class A Amateur Radio Licence holder (callsign G4HHU) with an interest in aerials, I would never trust my life to an aerial of less than professional construction.

Antenna Choice

The antenna you choose is obviously greatly influenced by the type of boat you drive, but you can never escape the basic tenet that a good, big aerial will always beat a good little one. The massive, vertical 'whips' seen on warships and mega-yachts, will always out-perform the smaller yacht aerials. They are many times more efficient.

Once you come down to normal yacht and sports boat, or RIB antennae, there is not really much difference in the performance of the following three basic types:

1. The Fibreglass Whip is popular because it is light and its outside is mostly constructed of a non-metallic substance, which is highly resistant to the corrosive effects of salt-spray. It also offers the option of encapsulating some of the connections beyond the reach of corrosion. Its downside is its vulnerability to snapping.
2. The Stainless Steel Whip is an equal performer and can often be made much slimmer and so have little windage. It is also of light weight and high corrosion resistance. Some models encapsulate the base connections, whilst others recognise that an owner might need to disconnect the unit, or will wish to take it apart from time to time to get the inevitable verdigris off the terminals. It is swings and roundabouts.
3. The Helical Winding, sometimes called the rubber duck, is also a viable option in spite of its insignificant appearance at the top of a yacht mast. In physical radio terms, it is little different from the vertical whip in length, but the active part is wound around an inert rod to make a coil inside a 'rubber' coating, which is very flexible and has practically zero windage.

Many yachtsmen disparage this sort of antenna, probably because it does not look 'flash' enough. They tend to forget that most of our communication is very short-range, so we are generally over-gunned. If you ever away. But this range was certainly enhanced by the weather.

Antenna Altitude

This is also a major factor. Returning to the 'line of sight' limitation and the apparent 1,200-foot mountain, which the Earth's curvature creates between Devon and Brittany, it is easy to appreciate that an aerial at the top of a 30-metre mast, or perched at 300 metres on a cliff top, will get a better 'look' over the horizon than one on the transom of a sports boat at sea-level. Equally, the antenna sitting on the mast of a tanker, which you often see above the horizon before you can discern the hull, can send a signal 'down' to an aerial at sea-level and receive from it.

These facts explain why you often only hear one half of a radio conversation, that is, one of the correspondents is 'line of sight' from you, but the other's antenna is hidden over your horizon, or is screened by an intervening headland. It also answers the often asked question why you hear HM Coastguard make the initial contact and then hear no more. The service has omnidirectional aerials on very high points, plus remote aerials at a distance. To improve reception and to cut interference, the contact is continued on the antenna most local to the station being worked.

Atmospheric Conditions

These are the greatest contributor to and inhibitor of VHF range. As already stated, VHF radio energy is line of sight, that is, if the

1.3 The stubby aerial is a helically-wound wire inside a rubber sheath.

have to un-ship the yacht's mast, the toughness of the 'rubber duck' is a great comfort. My own boats (yacht and RIB) have used them for fifteen years without feeling disadvantaged – even when talking to Portland Coastguard from Alderney, some fifty miles

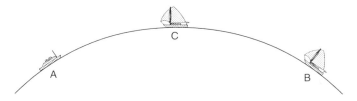

1.4 Boats A and B can both hear vessel C, but cannot hear each other.

tip of one antenna can be seen from the other, they can communicate. When atmospheric pressure is very high, the radio wave characteristics are slightly altered and induce ducting; that is, it follows the curvature of the Earth.

It is under such conditions that you hear the Humber Coastguard in the Solent and a motor yacht in Poole has talked to one in Treguier, even though the shape of the globe puts that famous equivalent of a 1,200-foot mountain between them.

The Fifth Factor

Having listed four TX and RX factors, there is a fifth. The quality of the receiver has a part to play. Some cheaper receivers have less good circuitry and are considerably 'deafer' than good quality gear. If your antenna is developing green contacts and solder joints and brown wire, you will also be well down in reception capability.

From Ground Rules to Cheque Book

If you understand what is happening when VHF radio is operated, you are in a better position to slice through the salesman's spiel and to get a radio suitable for your boat and for your wallet. Modern rigs have so many features and functions that this rapid patter can leave you totally brain-numbed, unless you know (a) what is essential, (b) what is desirable and (c) what is relatively useless, but has been incorporated because the chips and boards used in construction have spare capacity and design engineers do not like to leave it unoccupied.

Before you actually go shopping for a fixed VHF radio, it pays to do the maximum amount of research – which involves little more than reading the brochures and asking some sharp questions.

Type Approval is essential. This means that the radio has been submitted for official testing and has passed the required levels of

frequency stability and the rejection and suppression of spurious noise (that is, it does not interfere with hospital equipment or aircraft computers) and has adequate protection from the environment in order to be long-lasting and safe.

Getting Type Approval is a long-winded and costly procedure, so some distributors and manufacturers do not bother. This especially applies to clones and cheaper rigs imported from a variety of overseas countries. The vendors shelter behind that quirk in the law which makes it an offence to be caught using such equipment, but it is not technically illegal to offer it for sale. (Some shops have been prosecuted for incitement to commit a crime, but this is difficult to prove and is a deterrent which is not used much.) The language and practicality of Type Approval are more fully explained in the section covering radio law (p 22).

More recently, when boat owners apply for a ship's radio licence, they are asked to state the type of radio installed and the licence will not be issued if it is not type-approved. This is open to so much abuse as to be as laughable as are all the other arguments for the ridiculous annual £22 VHF radio licence fee, for which the seafarer seems to get very, very little.

The obligatory channels CH 16 (international calling and distress) and CH 06 (the primary inter-ship frequency) must be fitted by law. No VHF radio that I have ever seen has ever been offered without them. The only exception would be a very old crystal-controlled set where the crystals for TX and RX have been removed and sold separately, or their slots have been used for a CB, amateur bands or some other very esoteric frequency.

Low and high power option is generally standard and switchable between 25 watts and 5 watts. Some rigs offer a 6-watt lower power option, but this small increase makes so little operational difference that it is never worth extra money and can be ignored in the salesman's patter. There are just a few fixed

1.5 Note fixed radios 1-watt/25-watt settings. We should use 1-watt more often.

rigs incorporating a 1-watt low power setting. If you frequently use your VHF to talk to other angling or diving boats, or you normally talk to other boats cruising in very close company, this mini power means that you do not interfere with others using the same channel and – more important if you want to protect news of where the fish are biting – means that the transmissions do not travel very far and that you retain a higher degree of privacy. We should all use the low power setting much more than is our wont.

All the usual CHs are present, that is, 1 to 28, CH 37 (M) CHs60 to 80 (M2). There may be a few others to bring the total to 55, but the total list contains some unusual and unusable frequencies (CHs). It is worth reminding ourselves that CH 70 is reserved for Global Maritime Distress and Safety System (GMDSS) working.

GMDSS means that a vessel's callsign and position are sent digitally on this reserved distress channel. It can be received and decoded by any properly equipped shore station or other vessel. Once the data have been passed, the traffic reverts to any other working channel, which could be CH 67 (normally called the Coastguard or Small Ship Safety channel) or any other nominated by the correspondents.

At the time of writing, there are very few VHF radios with the requisite panic button encrypted with the callsign and interfaced with a position finder. GMDSS is also only applicable to vessels over 300 tons. There is every likelihood that it will become optional for leisure sailors, but most Search and Rescue agencies have indicated that they will continue a round-the-clock listening watch on CH 16.

Dual watch, which basically stays on your chosen CH, but regularly flicks to 16 and locks on if there is a signal, is excellent. A deluxe version will operate dual watch on any two CHs chosen by the operator – say, 12 for harbour and 80 for the marina. You can create a triple watch if your radio has a user-programmable memory function. Then you could set yourself for CH 16, CH 67 and your club's agreed, inter-yacht cruising frequency.

Both marina CHs – M and 80 – are becoming standard, but you do need to check on what has actually been fitted. Very few radios display the actual frequencies, which are a bit confusing, so the channels (CHs) are usually shown by their sequential numbers, beginning from 0, which is HM Coastguard's private channel. There are a few which need special mention.

CH 80 is now the primary working CH for traffic between vessels and yacht harbours and marinas, with CH M (sometimes known as CH 37) as a stand-by for busy periods. There is also the slightly usual CH M2

(161.425 MHz) which is used by certain clubs for race control purposes, with CH M as the back-up.

These are useful and interesting to monitor and enable you to keep out of the way of crowded events. CH 67 is the Coastguard small ship safety CH, mostly used for local weather forecasts, but also sometimes used for actual Search and Rescue operations.

Memory scanning and user-selectable memory scanning, allowing you to store your most often used CHs and to scan them, are good features. The normal scannable memory capacity is ten CHs (occasionally twenty-four or more) which is plenty. You can set the rig to scan all ten, or block off a few and scan the most important.

Full CH scanning is always included, but do not be too impressed by what must be the most useless VHF feature yet invented. It takes an age to scan the full CH range and the receiver continually locks up on useless CHs, harmonics from computers and even the white noise created by its own circuitry. A number of petrol and diesel engines also induce radio frequency 'noise' and the scanner will often lock onto this and not move without either some knowledgeable button pushing, or by switching the set off for a few seconds.

Weather CHs can also be ignored when the salesman is talking. They are receiver-only slots designed for use in America, where the US Coastguard regularly puts out weather forecasts on CHs dedicated to particular regions.

Private channels always sound an attractive idea, but they are expensive and inconvenient to fit and only work if the other person also has the same frequency installed.

Some Common Sense Tips From Hard Experience

1. Most people speak with their mouth too close to the microphone and this induces all manner of 'mush' and breathing noises into this sensitive instrument. Holding the mike about 10 cm from your lips makes for better quality received audio – as does slower than normal speech.

2. The 'over and out' fiasco still exists in spite of derisory publicity. The word 'over' means that you are passing transmission over to the other party and that you expect a reply. 'Out' indicates that you consider the conversation to be at an end and that no reply is expected. Thus, 'over and out' is a confusing nonsense.

3. It is good operating technique to leave a pause between RX and the next TX, not just to check that your correspondent has not added a postscript, but in case anybody wants to cut in with emergency traffic, or useful information.

4. When changing from 16 to a working channel, ask your caller to stand by whilst you check that the frequency is unoccupied at your end. Just listen for a few seconds. Remember that the station who nominates the channel is generally the second to speak. If you are asked to move to Channel 06, you announce your presence as soon as you get there and have noted that it is clear. Simply say something like 'This is Nonsuch on channel six' so that your correspondent knows that you are there and that they have actually engaged the agreed channel.

5. Ensure that your radio has a proper microphone stowage clip. Each summer, there is a spate of cases when Channel 16 is blocked by white noise created when somebody has stuffed a microphone onto a shelf and the push-to-talk button is jammed in the transmit position.

6. Use low power whenever possible.

7. If you are cruising in company, agree a working channel before you set off. You can then put this in dual watch or,

when you wish the other club member to switch to it, merely say 'Change channel' or use the more military 'Chop channel'.

8. Always end your transmission with the appropriate hand-over word, or use one of the very clear, acceptable phrases like 'Go ahead'.

9. If you are going well off-shore, it is wise to advise HM Coastguard (and to tell them when you get there) but for a ten-mile passage along the coast on a day when there are plenty of other yachts about, this is not necessary and only causes more work. The classic joke is of the yacht telling the Coastguard that he is leaving his marina berth to go to the fuel jetty.

10. Formality pays. Such one-worders as 'Roger' and 'Affirmative' convey a very precise meaning and avoid ambiguity. This language has been arrived at from much experience and saves many misunderstandings.

Chapter 2

Talking Handbags –
The Portable VHF Radio

A handheld VHF radio invariably comes high on every boat owner's list of desirable essentials. Sheer novelty apart, the 'talking handbag' has many things going for it – back-up, emergency, versatility of use, earwigging when you are ashore and the security of taking it home with you. The portable VHF can be made to do much more than its small size suggests, but it also has a parallel list of limitations and confusions – especially about range, price, type approval and licences.

Let us be very clear from the outset that the small, lower-powered, small-antennaed handheld radio will never be a match for the fixed rig, squirting 25 watts of RF power out of an aerial high on a mast or a cliff top, but that does not mean that it is not worth having.

As discussed in the preceding chapter, a combination of physical size and the laws of radio physics dictate that a radio at twice the price will not go twice as far and one with a small aerial will not compete with a big one. This knowledge should be part of your ammunition when you negotiate with sales people, who will often try to baffle you with exaggerated blurb and 'speed talk' rather than the facts above.

2.1 The family of handheld VHF radios.

2.2 The combined speaker and microphone is a worthwhile accessory.

Why Buy?

Let us, for a moment, forget the legal and licensing complexities of purchasing and using a handheld VHF (HHVHF) radio and concentrate on those practicalities which make our own boat's pair of portables the envy of other cruising friends.

The main, initial reason for acquisition always seems to be sea safety and falls under the umbrella that a good boat has two of everything. So, if your main radio goes on the blink, you have a back-up and it would always be there if you ever had to abandon ship. For these philosophies to be valid, the portable must be made capable of firing through the ship's main aerial and should be in a panic bag, kept ready-packed, in a very accessible place, ready to toss into the life-raft. Happily, most of us are less pessimistic and less adventurous about where and when we cruise, so we see other uses for the reserve radio.

My own has often served as the main radio when running our rigid hull inflatable as a club rescue boat, as a dive taxi and for other harbour odd jobs. For short range communication it is very adequate and its lower power avoids causing interference to others using the more popular channels.

On the motor sailer, when underway, it serves to monitor channels extra to those being followed on the main radio's dual watch settings. Very often the main rig is set for 16 and the marina channel, whilst its little brother monitors the harbour and pilot frequencies advising that the *QE Two*, or some other monster, is about to interfere with my passage up Southampton Water. Occasionally it follows Search and Rescue traffic on Channel 67, or keeps an eye on adjacent yachting and power boat events working Channel 10.

Using a separate VHF in the dinghy is a moot point with the radio licensing authorities, but when we are conning our way into a strange and rocky anchorage, or when we are helping another boat with a problem and even when the dinghy is away from the parent boat on an angling trip, to have a system of mobile communication makes very sound sense.

A boat travelling, say, through the French canals will find many uses for the HHVHF, even if a main radio jury antenna has not been rigged to compensate for the mast being along the deck to pass under bridges. Many canal travellers have bicycles and use them to send the warp and lock operating party ahead of the boat in preparation. If they can advise the boat of the state of the lock occupation and opening, they can make life a bit safer as well as saving themselves a lot of time and trouble.

Other skippers will have other uses even extra to keeping an ear on things when they are ashore.

Going Out to Buy – the Pre-purchase Check-off List

Actually buying a handheld radio has always been something of a minefield in which the guiding sales person is often as under-informed as the purchaser. There are, firstly, a number of misconceptions about cost.

The more expensive radio gets its higher price tag for a number of reasons, but it is not true to say that a radio costing twice as much will have twice as many features, or that it will send its signals twice as far.

Some manufacturers deliberately keep their prices high because they have an exaggerated opinion of their product's comparative value and retain a high price for reasons of snobbery and greed. They justify this with the cost of research and development and getting Type Approval and that they are suppliers to the armed services and some of the national Search and Rescue agencies. Such contracts do not necessarily imply superiority and the suppliers never add that these agencies hunt around and twist arms for the best bargains, just like the rest of us, and that they rarely pay shop prices for equipment. *Qui s'excuse, s'accuse* because there are some good rigs about at very sensible prices. You will not get twice as much from a HHVHF listed at £500 as you will from a good one priced £250 and available at £200 or less from discount outlets.

Robust construction and waterproofing are amongst the principal factors dictating price and they tend to influence each other. A HHVHF gets a very rough life of being pushed into damp lockers and falling off shelves, so the tougher you can afford, the better. When you handle a proposed purchase, if it feels right, it generally is right, but at minimum go for a rig which is water-protected, or splashproof. Many TCVRs claim to be splashproof, but the weak points are the seals on the push buttons. Again, if it looks right and feels right . . .

Full waterproofing costs more money, but the market is getting much better. You can

2.3 Full waterproofing costs money. The Navico is expensive but effective.

pay £500+ for a totally waterproof rig, but some of the new Japanese and American companies (Icom and Humminbird especially) are leading the trade in the direction we want it to go, that is, total HHVHF waterproofing at a price which the amateur can justify. Often, you can persuade a seller to include something like the Aquaman AQ2 or Radiomate waterproof bag as part of the deal. These products have been around for many years, so they are tried and trusted, but are easier to use if your TCVR has a front mounted keypad. That puts this high up the list of criteria for choice.

Features and Functions

Such physical, external features contribute heavily to manufacturing costs but – again – things are always getting better. The availability of cheap and powerful chips has made it easy to incorporate plenty of operating functions, so the top and middle models in price and quality are acquiring a standard list of things which they can do.

You can assume that a squelch control and CH 16 rapid access button are standard, then look for:

The Good, The Bad and The Useless.

Good rigs have a front-mounted keyboard with a screen to be readable in all light conditions. If you are a night-user, look for back-lighting which switches itself off after a set period of time. Without this feature, the light can be turned on by accident and is not really visible in daylight, so it could run for several hours and effectively reduce your battery life by half.

There are also some features to be avoided:

- Tiny, top-mounted knobs for changing channel and a very small channel number display. Such controls are difficult to operate with cold, wet hands, or when wearing gloves and the read-out is too small for the

2.4 Good layout of screen and keypad.

comfort of that 40 per cent of the population who need reading glasses.

- Banks of individually rechargeable AA batteries are a weak link and radios which use non-standard aerial connectors are a disaster. I recently lost my stubby antenna in Andraitx (Balearics) but because my HHVHF has a standard BNC connector, I was able to get a replacement for about £8.50, even in such a small town. Another radio has a special screw-thread base to the antenna. If I lose that one, the retailer demands £45 for a replacement.

We tend to be attracted by a radio specification's gimmicky electronic features, but the battery is the real guts of any portable radio system. The best power supplies are slide-off nicads, which can be charged when disconnected from the TCVR and you are using the second battery. Many newcomers are sensibly persuaded to have a second rechargeable battery and think that they will be able to leave this on charge (possibly from the boat's 12v supply, or via a voltage inverter) whilst they continue to run the rig. Unfortunately, some models do not have a separate battery connector, so can only be recharged when attached to the radio body. Because the charging lead disconnects the RX/TX circuitry, the radio is inoperable whilst the second battery is being revitalised. In some cases this can put it out of commission for twelve hours.

Some models change their output power by using a different battery, but the length of time a radio can be used is totally dependent on battery capacity and this is at the mercy of how the rig is used. On stand-by (that is, in receive-only mode) all batteries will last for several hours, but transmission (especially on High Power) is a big drain. ICOM for example market eleven different rechargeable batteries for their handheld radios alone, so the only sensible approach is to ask your local electronics supplier to show you the

The Law

1. If the HHVHF is your boat's only transmitting radio, you will need a Ship's Radio Licence costing £22 per year. Each ship/boat is allocated an official callsign – like MBNU9.

2. The HHVHF can be operated on the same boat as a secondary radio under the ship's licence. In law, independent use in the dinghy should require another ship's licence.

3. The operator must have a VHF Operator's Certificate of Competence, costing £25 for life and usually gained following a one-day course.

4. The only exception to (3) is a person operating properly licensed equipment under the direct supervision of a licensee.

5. In order to get a Ship's Radio Licence, the vessel must be fitted with equipment which is Type Approved by passing UK tests. For normal leisure-use the current approval codes are MPT1251/1252, which will soon be the European ES standard.

6. Type Approval is costly to obtain, so some distributors of excellent equipment do not bother. This creates the confusing anomaly that it is not illegal to sell, or to buy, non-Type Approved equipment, but it is a reportable offence to be caught using it.

VHF Speak and Reading the Spec

Frequency is the number of pulses per second of radio energy pushed away from the antenna and is quoted in millions (Mega) and thousands (Kilo) of Hertz. For marine VHF the lowest frequency used is 156 million (156.00 MHz). CH 16 is 156.800 MHz. The 800 KHz difference between CH 0 (156 MHz) and CH 16 gives channel spacings of 50 KHz.

Channel really means the same as frequency, but makes for smaller numbers. There is some confusion here because, for example, CH 8 is 156.400 MHz but 156.425 MHz is allocated to CH 68. Early VHF radio had poor frequency stability, so needed 50 KHz separation to prevent inter-channel interference. Modern rigs will tolerate 25 KHz and extra channels were put on the frequencies in-between. Soon 12.5 KHz will be possible.

Squelch is the internal noise created by the radio's own circuitry and other factors. This can be attenuated (diminished) by a control set so that only signals stronger than this noise will be heard at the loudspeaker. All radios have a squelch control.

Signal to Noise ratio is a comparison between 'squelch' and 'received signal' and a good signal has a high ratio. The comparative figure is quoted in decibels (or Db) which – simplistically – is a logarithmic system of comparing sounds in units of ten.

Noise/Spurii Rejection is also quoted in Db and quantifies how finely tuned the circuitry is made, that is, it accepts the signals for which each CH is tuned, but rejects others even if they are quite close. There is also a mechanism to reduce internal noise plus spurious signals from computers and even other radios transmitting on harmonics (any frequency which is a whole number multiple of the one you are using).

Simplex is any CH dedicated to single-operator use. If both parties speak at the same time they blot each other out. Some CHs are **Duplex** (for example, 26) with TX and RX on different frequencies and allowing both parties to hear whilst talking. There is no need to say 'over' to clear the line.

price and performance figures for a good second battery. In this respect, amateur radio shops (most of whom also sell marine equipment) are often better informed than a general ship chandler.

Ask about the charging time and method. In most cases, the charger supplied will be mains current (AC) operated, which is usually acceptable, but not much good if your boat is doing an extended cruise, or if you are going on holiday and wish to recharge the radio battery from the car, or the boat 12v supply. Charging time varies from fifteen to twenty-four hours and some battery models can be over-charged. There is no substitute for asking questions and getting answers verified from the distributor's specification sheets. There are also a number of HHVHF rigs about with a five-hour rapid charger.

I am a big fan of portable VHF radios which can also be run from an external 12v supply. I get a lot of versatile use from one of my own coupled to a marine portable power pack (LVM manufacture one), or from a 10-ampere-hour battery, which is normally sold as a back-up to burglar alarms. Motorcycle dealers also sell a solid, jelly-filled battery which is suitable. In addition to the radio, these extra, highly portable power sources can have a dozen other on-board uses – from pumping diesel and running a soldering iron to powering a riding light.

You could use this isolated power supply set-up as your sole communications facility, which would be especially good for an outboard motor-powered boat where, to be really safe, you should switch off your radio (and any other electronics) when you start up in order to protect the circuitry from the huge voltage spikes which some engines emit.

Extra Accessories Mean Extra Cash

Most ranges of HHVHF have a separate catalogue of optional extras. The rule is always to ask the price before you buy and to hasten slowly – you can always add them one at a time when you get the wisdom of use and experience. My own most practical accessories have been:

1. Second battery pack (£20).
2. 12v lead (£8.50).
3. Rapid charger (£22).
4. Fist mike/speaker, so that the rig can go in the pocket of my waterproofs and the extension can be held close to the ear for better audio strength (£35).
5. Leather case (£15).

A useful accessory is a 6-foot extension lead with both ends terminating in PL259 plugs. One end goes into the adapter above; the other connects to the ship's aerial via a PL259 back-to-back connector. This makes the HHVHF more usable on the parent ship and will also fit an emergency antenna. The fittings cost about £1.80 each at Tandy, Radio Shack or any ham radio retailer.

Chapter 3

More Powerful Communications

In the field of leisure marine activity, the term SSB remains a bit of a mystery and gives a certain cachet to those skippers who have installed a marine single side band transceiver and actually know how it works. It marks them out as serious, off-shore cruisers, with some very special knowledge and equipment. I was once at one of those happy hour cockpit parties, where all the ladies were in total awe of one wife who constantly boasted 'I have an SSB licence'.

Therefore, let us begin to clear away those factors which have given marine SSB radio the reputation of being a black art, which it does not really merit.

In most discussions, the mariner's appreciation of radio is simplified to 'How far does it go?' If you wish to send your messages to receivers further afield, you need to use a lower frequency and be able to marry-up time of day with the frequency band you have selected – or, more accurately, vice versa.

Professionals adopt roughly defined distance conventions in which:

- Ultra High Frequency (UHF) is used – mostly by the military – for short distances and for communications via satellites. Because there is no blocking terrain, or high buildings in the line of sight close to the transmitter, low power UHF signals can cover enormous distances out into space and back. UHF is generally quoted as being any frequency over 200 MegaHertz. Remember that Channel 16 VHF is 156.8 MHz and that GPS signals are at frequencies high enough to be at near microwave level.

- Very High Frequency (VHF) radio is normally line of sight and legally limited to 25 watts output. Power is less important than aerial efficiency and 30 miles is the average capture zone. The conventions place VHF in the 30–300 MHz band.

- Medium Frequency (MF) radio waves are in the spectrum 0.3 MHz or 300 Kilocycles to 3.0 MHz and go further because they follow the curvature of the earth. Marine users of this band are confined to an output power of 400 watts maximum. There is a rule of thumb that an efficient antenna will radiate a signal for about 0.75 nautical miles per watt of output. Thus, if your equipment can develop and transmit the full power, you can expect a range of about 300 miles. Because gear is rarely as efficient as the brochures claim, the skipper who settles for an MF range of 250 miles will not be disappointed. This band is sub-divided into several special segments, many of which are occupied by local radio broadcast stations. For the mariner, the most important frequencies are 518 KHz, which is dedicated to the Navtex service, and 2182 KHz, which is the international calling and distress frequency.

• High Frequency (HF) radio signals can be made to travel all the way around the world. The spectrum 3 MHz to 30 MHz is where specialised aerials and favourable atmospheric conditions are much more important than raw output power. Using a short whip mounted on the davits of a ten-metre yacht, I frequently make contact with fellow radio hams in America when our boat is in the Mediterranean and have contacted Australia from an un-obtrusive length of wire just a few centimetres clear of the back wall of our house. HF signals travel far because they are reflected back to Earth from the ionospheric layer of particles circling roughly 200 miles above us. Using a directional beam antenna, it is possible for, say, a UK radio ham to speak to one in Greece by directing the signals west so that they take the long path right around the world. The HF spectrum must be used for all distances in excess of 300 nautical miles.

This background information is useful to the yacht skipper who ventures a little further afield. It enables him to understand why he did not receive a Navtex broadcast from Niton Radio, because he was in a certain location, or why his expensive SSB set seems to perform better at night than during the day.

SSB equipment should be seen as having three components:

1. The expensive transceiver.
2. The comparatively inexpensive antenna
3. Enough operator knowledge to get a licence.

The SSB transceiver has become much more sophisticated over the past decade. More exactly, it has become more complex on the inside, but the external controls have

3.1 Typical marine SSB radio transceiver.

become much simpler to use. The reasons for this interior improvement are general progress and much better engineering. A significant portion of this modernisation has been forced onto manufacturers by various legislative acts governing Electromagnetic Compatibility (EMC). These directives are designed to prevent differing types of electrical equipment from causing interference to each other. If you have ever tried to run a radio close to a computer, you will have noticed a whining noise. Some computers themselves are also affected by certain types of radio noise – that is, those false signals and their harmonics straying into other circuits. On my own boat, I cannot transmit on the amateur bands rig without causing all the LED switches to light up, the circuit monitor to sprout indecipherable figures and the autopilot to go completely loopy.

The solution to most of these maladies is improved screening of output components from other parts of the radio. This is achieved by putting them in their own internal metal boxed compartments, or by filtering off and cancelling out noise by clever use of capacitors. These days, there are not so many bare wires to act as internal aerials and the insulation of joints and connections is also much better. This means that unwanted signals are better imprisoned to keep them away from where they can cause mischief.

This internal improvement has also made for greater transceiver stability, that is, the frequency does not slide a few cycles (Hertz) up or down as the circuitry becomes warmer. This, in turn, has enabled a more extensive use of fixed channels, with no danger that they will stray into each other.

Prior to 1982, ship HF/MF radios could be tuned to any frequency on the band. Since then, however, the long-distance rigs have been canalised, that is, most of them will only operate on certain designated frequencies, or channels. This is policed by the system of Type Approval, which means that a model has been rigorously tested and proved to be compliant with all the directives for power,

frequency stability and inability to stray out of the marine band whilst in transmission mode.

In spite of this progress, there remain a few atmospheric and interference factors which can cause a receiver signal to be slightly down in clearness, but on most sets these can be adjusted and partially eliminated by a fine-tuning clarifier knob.

Every ship radio must be licensed and an annual fee is payable. The authorities will only license Type Approved equipment and there are heavy fines for using so-called pirate rigs.

The operators must also have a licence proving that they are competent. This is granted against a one-off, for life fee and follows passing an exam which is just a little more difficult than the VHF test, but not much more difficult. It leads to the granting of what used to be called the radio Restricted Certificate of Competence – otherwise known as the SSB licence.

Since the advent of GMDSS (explained in Chapter 1) the syllabus for this piece of paper has been changed and it is now, more sensibly, called the CEPT Long Range Radio Telephone Certificate, which is discussed in detail in the information box at the end of this chapter. CEPT is an acronym for the French language title of The European Conference of Postal and Telecommunications Administration, which regularly meets to make international agreements covering use of the various radio spectra.

It is a quirk of the law that any other (unlicensed) person aboard the vessel can use the VHF radio, or the much more powerful HF radio, provided that they are under the supervision of a licence holder. Without this provision, no passenger on a cruise liner would be able to make calls to shore via the radio telephone service. But even this is simplified by putting the radio into duplex mode.

Simplex operation needs just one frequency (or channel) and one antenna. It means that the correspondents must take it in turns to speak, because their radio sets cannot simultaneously transmit and receive. VHF users soon get to realise that if they hold down the push-to-talk button on the microphone, the receive side of the transceiver is disabled and no incoming signals can be heard. The two participants signify that they have finished talking and are ready to listen by using the word 'over', which means 'I am passing transmission over to you and am listening for the expected reply'.

Duplex operation makes an SSB (or other) radio behave like a telephone line, along which both parties can speak and listen at the same time. It requires a radio constructed to keep the receive circuits open on the authorised duplex channels, even though the transmit button is keyed. It also needs twin aerials and these must be sited sufficiently far apart to prevent the transmission energy from totally swamping the receive side. Good duplex is only really feasible on mega yachts.

Semi-duplex is not much seen nowadays, but some older rigs still use two frequencies and can manage duplex conversations as long as, say, the Coast Radio Station has been forewarned. Radio amateurs do something similar to avoid local interference by operating in split frequency mode, that is, they transmit and receive on different frequencies.

The antenna is as important to marine SSB as it is to getting good performance from the amateur bands radio, which it closely resembles. The principles are also similar. If you merely wish to receive radio signals, almost any length of wire will work, but the longer the wire the better the reception. Having said this, you will get improved results by using a properly-tuned aerial, that is, one which is the correct resonant length for the frequency in use.

The simplest way to get a very efficient antenna is to have your SSB installation done by a professional, who could either advise a long, fibreglass whip, or will install a separate wire dipole. The alternative most often employed is to isolate a length of the backstay by inserting top and bottom insulators and processing the signals via an antenna tuning unit (ATU).

The basic antenna for all radio frequencies is a half wave dipole. This is a very explicit title telling us that its length must be half of a wavelength and split into two poles, or halves.

The formula for calculating half wave dipole length is:

$$150/\text{frequency (MHz) metres or}$$
$$492/\text{frequency}$$
$$\text{(MHz) feet.}$$

Thus an antenna for the calling and distress frequency 2182 MHz is:

$$150/2.182 = 68.7 \text{ metres.}$$

This an impossible length for a boat, which is why we need the ATU.

Obviously, if you 'cut' an aerial for a specific frequency, it will not work well on a different wavelength. This is another reason for the ATU, which electronically alters the apparent length of wire in order to 'kid' the radio that it has physically changed.

Most ATUs are very simple to use and rely on just two rotary controls, for tune and load. They are adjusted until the dial indicators

3.2 A couple of ATU units suitable for marine use.

CEPT Long Range Radiotelephone Certificate (examination requirements)

Examination Syllabus for the CEPT LRC for vessels not subject to Compulsory Fit under the SOLAS Convention.

The examination should consist of theoretical and practical tests and should include at least:

1. **General knowledge of Radio Communications in the Marine Mobile Service**
    The general principles and basic features of the maritime mobile service.

2. **Detailed Practical Knowledge and Ability to use Radio Equipment**
    The VHF radio installation. Use VHF equipment in practice.
    The MF/HF radio installation. Use MF/HF equipment in practice.
    Purpose and use of Digital Selective Calling (DSC) facilities.

3. **Operational Procedures of the GMDSS and Detailed Practical Operation of GMDSS Subsystems and Equipment Appropriate to Non-SOLAS Vessels**
    Basic introduction to Global Maritime Distress and Safety system (GMDSS) procedures C2.
    Distress, urgency and safety communication procedures in the GMDSS.
    Distress, urgency and safety communication procedures by radiotelephony in the old distress and safety system.
    Protection of distress frequencies.
    Maritime Safety Information (MSI) systems in the GMDSS.
    Alerting and Locating Signals in the GMDSS.

4. **Miscellaneous Skills and Operational Procedures for Radiotelephone Communications**
    Ability to exchange communications relevant to the safety of life at *sea*.
    Obligatory procedures and practices.
    Practical and theoretical knowledge of radiotelephone procedures.

---

show the minimum of radio energy being reflected back into the black box and the maximum being pushed up the antenna feeder. These indicators always work in harmony with each other, that is, as the VSWR (roughly meaning reflected energy) comes down, so the output power always goes up.

Those of us with shallow pockets write down the tune and load dial settings for all our most often-used frequencies, so that we can always come back to them without testing by putting up a carrier wave, or the even more anti-social method of blowing into the microphone to create an output. If your pocket is deeper, there are now several varieties of smart ATU which can tune almost any length of wire to transmission resonance and can remember a couple of hundred settings.

As explained, a simple practical aerial can be made by having a professional insert the insulators into the boat's backstay, then adding a DIY feeder. This is often made by attaching a coaxial cable to the backstay with two or three jubilee clips, or other crimpers. The coaxial is then fed into the ATU by a normal plug.

Get the ATU as close to the antenna as space will physically allow, even if you are using a very low-loss coaxial feeder. The shorter the feeder, the smaller the loss in signal strength. Doing this might mean that you will install a separate ATU control box at the chart table, but this is smaller and more convenient than the ATU unit itself.

The function of the ATU is now to persuade the backstay that it is one half of a dipole and so, therefore, a quarter of a wavelength long. The other half of our half wave dipole is ground, or earth which normally means the actual soil itself, but on boats means the sea. Its antenna component is added by connecting the radio itself to ground from a dedicated connector on the back of the set. It sounds like a contradiction of terms, but the sea makes a super radio ground plane, especially if the boat is equipped with a proper earthing plate (not to be confused with sacrificial anodes).

There is something of a bonus here, because not only does the sea make a super 'earth', but it is also a very efficient reflector of radio signals back up into the ether. This phenomenon partly explains why my stainless steel whip antennae work much better on the boat than they do on the car, for which they were originally designed.

A word of warning is appropriate to any boat owner installing his own SSB aerial. Make sure that the lower insulator is high enough to prevent anybody touching the active part of the backstay when the radio is being used in transmission mode. Radio frequency energy is very powerful stuff and can give RF burns to the careless.

Alternative aerials are often sought by people like myself who are old-fashioned enough to think simplistically. To us, one piece of apparatus equals one function. Even though I do not know of an instance where a radio insulator has been the cause of backstay failure, my own philosophy leads me away from this, which means that I must either stay with my (less efficient) whips, or accept some extra wire strung around the masts of our ketch. There are many available designs, which can be quickly constructed from ordinary insulated wire and a length of coaxial cable, or 300-ohm ribbon feeder, which is much lighter.

On the amateur radio shelf of my bookcase, I have about a dozen volumes devoted to aerials and how to make them. Most of this material could be adapted to the construction of marine SSB radiators and receivers because some of the frequencies are very close. This fact is mentioned not so much for the pride of my literary collection, but to re-emphasise the point that if you buy the most expensive SSB radio in the world, but give it an inefficient antenna, you would do better to leave the money in the bank.

Chapter 4

Amateur Radio

Amateur radio adds such an interesting extra to my cruising life that the boat would be much poorer without it. There was a day in Formentera when Roger rowed over to thank me for a weather forecast, which he had heard me get and repeat on the UK Maritime Mobile net. He and his wife then stayed for a drink and have since become our good friends. Or there is Tom (callsign G4MXX) whose 14.303 MHz, long distance signal surprisingly reached us from an adjacent bay, so came round for the best barbecue of the year. We heard a US radio ham worrying that he was short of drinking water and were able to direct him to an abandoned building site only 200 yards away from his anchorage and where he got gallons of Balearic gold-free, drinkable water. We were about 250 miles away at the time, but had found the drinking hole the year previously. After this, there was Gilbert (F5JEO) with whom we made amateur radio VHF contact on 144.5 MHz (2-metre band) and who took us to his Bordeaux home and the shops, then offered us the use of the workshop on the warship *Colbert* do some repairs.

This is just one shelf from a vast library illustrating that Colin Jones is just another anonymous cruiser skipper, but as G4HHU, or Gee Four Double Aitch You, he is friendly with a healthy sprinkling of the 80,000-plus licensed radio amateurs in the UK alone and is also recognised by ten times that number who listen to our nets and other radio traffic.

There are plenty of cruising reasons for enjoying all facets of amateur radio:

1. Like Roger, above, who just listens for useful information and for pleasure.
2. To belong to Tom's great circle of friends, who can talk boat-to-boat and to shore from cruising grounds everywhere.
3. For the cruising practicality of our water diviner's act from 300 miles away.
4. For Gilbert and international amity.

Oddly, sea safety is at the forefront of this rationale. It happens that radio hams help with problems, but so rarely in comparison to better search and rescue facilities that it would not be high on my list of reasons for becoming a 'ham'. For most of us, ham radio is primarily useful fun.

Who Are These Freaks?

So, who are these people who speak an esoteric shorthand of qth, qsl, g5rv and propagation? Firstly, they admit to playing ham radio, but do not always like being called a Radio Ham since the gutter press began using the term to identify unlicensed weirdos who have cheap scanners and get involved in eavesdropping on mobile telephones and other privacies.

Nor should this friendly, qualified bunch be confused with users of Citizens' Band radio, marine SSB sets, or holders of the marine VHF restricted radio certificate. The dedicated radio enthusiast will have undertaken a course of study and will have passed the comprehensive, written City and Guilds Radio Amateur Examination (held twice a year) to be granted a Class B licence to transmit on frequencies above 50 MHz. This is relatively low power and short range stuff, unless you get into the highly technical moon bounce and meteor scatter scene.

Tests and Licences

In order to talk to friends in Australia and America, you need the legal power and lower operating frequencies open to Class A licence holders, who have additionally passed a Morse code test at twelve words a minute. There are many local Morse examiners and the RAE is held at a number of centres, including any UK embassy/consulate.

We are frequently asked why, when the air is free, should one need all this exam aggro to use it? The answer is that free access is open to even more abuse than that perpetrated by those swearers, Channel 16 monopolisers, idiots and music players you hear on marine VHF and CB, where transmission permission can almost be obtained 'on the nod'. If you are going to be let loose with power to send signals right around the world, you must have enough competence not to endanger others by straying onto air bands, or to cut out hospital equipment, or to give offence to listeners. If, for instance, I tune my main aerial badly, I can break in on the telephone and wipe out the TV reception for 400 yards around.

The Morse test is sometimes seen as an anachronism, but there needs to be some way of limiting the number of users of an already crowded HF radio spectrum, otherwise we get into the muddle of, say, Japan, where access is too easy, so nobody can get a clear, legitimate frequency. At the moment, the hurdle is a Morse test and even though this transmission mode is losing military favour, it is still much used by radio amateurs because it carries greater distance with clarity and requires a very narrow frequency slot for effectiveness: many ships still use CW and my most reliable weather forecasts in the Mediterranean have been in Morse from Rome and France Meteo Toulouse.

The Radio Amateur Exam syllabus

The forty-five multiple choice questions cover the following topics:

- Receivers and receiving techniques
- Measurements
- Operating techniques
- Construction
- Licensing conditions
- Components, applications and units
- Propagation and antennae
- Station layout
- Safety

The fact remains that if you want to make all the friends which amateur radio implies and to have the twenty-four hours a day fun of playing it, you will need to pass the exams, but that need not be daunting. The RAE comprises a single one and a quarter hour test of forty-five multiple choice questions on a variety of topics, both technical and relating to the privilege and regulations involved in holding a licence. The very fact that there are about 80,000 licence holders in UK alone and that they come from all walks of life and all levels of schooling, income, accent, gender, colour, profession and age, is proof enough that the exam is fair.

The Ways in to the Fun

The usual way in is to get a copy of the Radio Society of Great Britain (RSGB) booklet 'How To Become a Radio Amateur', or to buy a 'Janet and John' level primer from an amateur radio shop and then attend one of the winter courses run by local education authorities, or by radio clubs. In my own case, the nearest course was too far away, so I had to work from books and tapes and ask (willing) enthusiasts to help. I am entirely non-technical, but I really wanted that licence, so I learned part of the syllabus by heart and made myself do thirty minutes Morse each day – as well as having tapes in the car.

The fun which I have had from the end result certainly justified the means. It has given me eighteen years of continuous pleasure and made me lasting friends just about everywhere I travel. At home, in the winter, I regularly meet other boat owners 'on the air' and we swap information and opinions and help each other solve boat problems. The same applies when we are cruising.

Typical of these was a boat in the Mediterranean transmitting wiring instructions for re-installing a repaired starter motor to the owner of a similar engine in the Baltic. In our own case, we were able to solve a problem of DIP switches and graphics for the owner of a bubblejet printer and our boat's computer is regularly fired up to give tidal information to yachts a hundred miles away.

Another way into the hobby is to begin as a Short Wave Listener (SWL). There are thousands of them and they regularly send me cards and letters to say that they have followed our progress throughout the cruising season. (They obtain my address from the annually up-dated UK Callsign book.) Listening is an excellent way of learning operating techniques and of getting an understanding of aerials, callsigns and radio language.

Special and Non-special Equipment

The equipment need not be expensive, nor elaborate. On my desk, I have a tiny Sony SW 7600G receiver running off batteries. Currently, I am listening to the International Police Amateur Radio Association net on 40 metres, just on the telescopic aerial. If I plug in a more powerful antenna, I shall hear Americans coming on as they play for an hour before going to work, then all the cruising boats. The Sony cost about £160 and replaced a slightly bulkier model bought for £100 second-hand.

A number of companies, such as the long-established Lowe Electronics, produce an excellent communications receiver and a suitable aerial for under £500. 'Com-

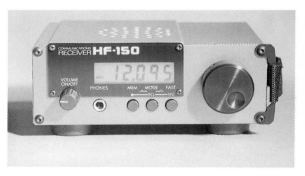

4.1 Lowe HF150 receiver.

4.2 The NASA Target HF bands receiver.

4.4 Very sophisticated amateur bands TCVR.

munications' implies that the radio will cover the frequency range 30 KHz to 30 MHz and be capable of switching between upper/lower sidebands – USB and LSB. This is so-called single side-band (SSB) working.

SSB gets around the problem that such low frequency pulsations as the human voice are audible, but they only travel short distances, whilst high frequencies have great linear range, but are inaudible. Radio transmission 'mounts' the low on the high by mixing them into a sine wave going above and below the nominal carrier frequency. To increase the practical output power, either Upper Side Band (USB) or Lower Side Band (LSB) is suppressed to give more penetration (and the compressed Donald Duck voice) effect to SSB, which needs a special set of circuitry to unscramble the mix. By convention, radio amateurs use USB for frequencies above 10 MHz and LSB for all below. This is a very simplistic explanation of a complex

but logical process and it should make you see why a tuition course is necessary. Safe radio implies more than just operating the set.

Many yacht owners who are determined to get a licence begin by listening on a full amateur bands transmitter (TX) cum receiver (RX) set, generally called a transceiver (TCVR). This puts out a massive 100 watts and even though it is blocked to work only the amateur bands, it is common knowledge that a single correct internal wire snip will open up the marine SSB bands too. This is illegal in commercial operation in some countries, which is why we did not tell you

4.5 The author's own large base station rig and the small TS50 which is an ideal boat station.

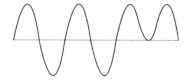

4.3 Full sine wave becoming SSB.

Radio Propagation

HF Radio propagation and range are controlled by an ionised layer (the ionosphere) whose height above earth and reflective powers vary according to the time of day and the season. Radio waves hit the layer and are reflected down to earth again – and can even bounce up and down again to give enormous range. Distance is also affected by the eleven-year sunspot cycle.

Frequency (metres)	Wavelength (mls/kms)	Distance*	Night Time Range* (also early am)
3.5–3.8	80	300/	1000/
7.0–8.0	40	750/	1500/
14–15	20	2000/	Worldwide**
21–25	15	3000/	Worldwide**
28–30	10	Worldwide but very patchy	

* Propagation improves in the direction of the sun.
**Falls off at about 2000 hours local.

that it happens everywhere (with VHF too).

Obtaining this sort of equipment, ready for when you have a Class A licence, is obviously more expensive in the short term, but brings tandem advantages. The popular ICOM 736 currently retails at about £1,650, but its 735 predecessor can be bought second-hand for £800 or less. On my home bench, I have a new all-singing Kenwood TS450S bought for £1,350. It is called a mobile rig, but is a bit lumpy, so my boat radio is the less sophisticated, but adequate and much smaller Kenwood TS50S, currently retailing at about £900 inclusive, but with an emerging used market. Before that, I had plenty of fun with an old £450 Yaesu FT747X. They all worked well and can all be found in *Practical Wireless* every month, or in any amateur radio shop.

Before you can receive or transmit properly, there are inevitably some extras, amongst which will be an antenna. Radio aficionados are fascinated by aerials, because they know that radio power is aerial power. As was mentioned in our discussion of VHF, if you have the best radio in the world and the worst aerial, you have the worst radio and

this syndrome is even more exaggerated when you are handling the higher power utilised on the amateur bands. The problem is that to be resonant (that is, to handle pulsations at a given rate/frequency) an aerial needs to be a very precise length. If this is wrong, the high-power energy does not get blasted away into the ether, but is reflected back down the wire and can return all sorts of 'funnies' back into an expensive radio as well as into the autopilot, computer, instruments, etc. In some instances this will even totally trash a very expensive rig in a few seconds. Again a simplistic explanation of a costly error and why you need to know what you are doing.

This resonant length changes for every frequency, but because constant physical alteration is impossible, it is done electronically, as we have already mentioned, by inserting into the line an antenna tuner unit (ATU) which will add about £70 to £250 to your bill, but will enable you to RX/TX on any length of wire. You know that one popular solution is to insert two heavy duty insulators into the backstay and to tape on a

Common International Callsign Prefixes

America	KA–KZ
Australia	VK
Canada	VE/VO/VY
Denmark	OZ
Finland	OH
France	F–FE
Germany	DA–DL
Gibraltar	ZB2
Holland	PA
Ireland	EI
Italy	I
Norway	LA/LB
Spain	EA
Switzerland	HE
UK	G

GM = Scotland, GW = Wales etc
EA6 = Balearics, IS = Sardinia etc
F/G4HHU= UK Station in France etc

Amateur Radio Shorthand

QRL	frequency is in use, please QSY
QRM	there is interference from another station
QRN	there is atmospheric interference
QRP	operating lower power
QRT	closing down
QRX	wait a moment
QSB	there is fading on the signal
QSL	the message has been received
QSO	a conversation; a contact
QSP	a relay by a third station
QSY	change frequency
CW	Morse (continuous wave)
YL	a young lady
XYL	the young lady you married
ROGER	message received and understood
SILENT KEY	person deceased

feeder coaxial to the ATU and ground. Others use a triatic stay between the masts, or erect a simple inverted-V dipole (two lengths of wire split at a T-shape insulator) and fed from the apex at the masthead by the inner and outer of a coaxial. My own usual antenna is a slim, commercial whip designed for mobile use on a car, but mounted on our stern davits. It lacks really huge power but, last year, I regularly worked America from Corsica and said my daily piece on the indispensable UK Maritime Mobile Net.

Nets and Schedules (SKEDS)

Net(work)s are agreed places on the dial where groups of like-minded 'hams' meet to chat and exchange information. There are nets for Esperanto, ex-RN personnel, Rotary,

Bretons and so on. For most of us, the best known is The UK Maritime Mobile net, which for the last twenty-five years has happened at 0800 and 1800 UTC/GMT every day of the year on 14.303 MHz USB. It was started to track a British boat across The Pond, but is now used as a meeting place by yachts of all nationalities, cruising everywhere – the Mediterranean, the Azores, the Caribbean, the Baltic and around UK. Even when I am ashore in winter, I find it compulsive listening.

Weather and forecasts are an important

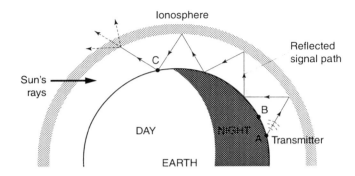

Ionosphere

Reflected
signal path

Sun's
rays

C

DAY   NIGHT

B

A   Transmitter

EARTH

4.6 The bounce effect of the ionosphere.

part of the information exchange orchestrated by the regular land-based controllers located in Surrey, in Humberside and from Flamborough Head.

Each of the controllers has weatherfax pulled by their ham radio gear (or comms receiver) onto a PC by special software and a demodulator cable. This equipment is easy to install on a yacht and many skippers use it to augment the control station information. Other boats simply give their location, actual weather (WX) conditions and barometric reading, which all adds up to a complete weather picture – available free of charge.

Vessels on passage call in to give their position and mostly to report 'all well on board'. Recently, however, 'The Net' was able to get assistance out to a sinking multi-hull and also monitored a crew with a sick engine and a very young baby fighting a gale into the Azores.

Most of us spend much more time listening than transmitting and are content to know where our friends have arrived. If we want to make contact, we QSY (change frequency) to chat without holding up the net but, more often, we simply relay greetings as we cannot hear the other station because they are too close – or too far away. You cannot play amateur radio well without a knowledge of propagation and why range changes with time and season. In the early morning, for example, you might hear America on 3.5 MHz, but by noon I can have problems establishing a Lyme Regis-to-

Yorkshire link on that frequency band, so we might need to change to 7 MHz – and so on.

There are several other English-speaking maritime mobile rendezvous, such as the Atlantic and Caribbean net, which did a tremendous job in collating information on the unfortunates who suffered Hurricane Luis. To find this net and its roaming contacts tune to 21.400 at 1300 hours. You will also be able to locate nets for boats from Germany, America and contacts speaking Flemish and Russian and so on. Even if they use their native tongue, you can always determine the country of origin by the first letters and figures of the callsigns. G and M are UK, F is France, K and others are USA, ON equals

Belgium and so on but they will all use the amateur radio lingua franca shorthand.

This is based on the Q code, which was designed to overcome language barriers by a question and answer letter group – usually in Morse. For example 'QTH?' asks 'What is your location?' The reply 'QTH (no question mark) Dieppe' is easily understood. 'QRM?' asks 'Are you being interfered with?' It begets an answer which has nothing to do with sexual harassment.

There is nowadays a pennant to show that a radio amateur, or SWL is aboard, but all 'ham' equipped boats have funny insulators and extra wires and long whip antennae. Not many of us are of the Tony Hancock image, but we all like people and talking about weather, radio and boats.

4.7 The international maritime mobile operator (or listener) pennant.

Chapter 5

Alternative Communications

Here is an entry from our ship's log cum diary.

Cherbourg, 19 May. The barometer has dropped 8mb in 2 hours and the wind gone beyond the 49 knots to which our instrument reads. The rain is icy. We really need to get home, but it would be stupid to go to sea in such weather and we have no wish to abandon the boat and return to England by ferry. We are stuck here, but we are not isolated. The mobile phone sits in the wheelhouse and occasionally chirps a business contact, so we have been able to stay dry, but have managed to give friends news of our safety and keep in touch with our clients. Here, the second of our talking handbags is a comfort. Out in an isolated bay, screened from VHF propagation, it could add another dimension to our boat efficiency and safety.

The yacht phone is not only here to stay, but is already being offered as part of a number of new boat packages and will increasingly play a major role in boat communications. Its very presence gives the freedom for a number of us to cruise and work at the same time. Why not? The mobile telephone takes nothing away from boating pleasures and security, but can enhance them. If you value periods of silence, you need not switch it on.

Even though we cruise in company with a cell phone, it will never replace – or even compete with – the VHF/MF radio for a number of reasons. There are times when it might (only might) fill in reception gaps and it does sometimes have a human contact certainty denied to VHF (which it technically closely resembles), so there is a very good chance that somebody will answer the call. But, even we gadgetophiles recognise that the mobfone – to coin a phrase – has its own limitations. Sense says that if you have one, carry it on the boat. Prudence counsels that it does not make you immortal.

We who go to sea need reliable communications for two main reasons: first, private, directed person-to-person contact; and secondly, good seamanship and safety. In trying to see the mobfone in context, you cannot avoid comparison with VHF and other radio forms. To get this comparison, or contest, between phone and radiophone picture in perspective, we are actually comparing like with like, because they are both radio transmitters (TX) and receivers (RX). They both raise questions of (a) that amalgam of range/efficiency/certainty of contact, (b) suitable equipment, (c) costs and (d) what you can use the equipment for. When they are 'in the picture', visitors to our motor-sailer, *Abemama*, always ask 'Does the mobile phone really work? What's in it for me? How do I get one?'

Effective Communication

Boat VHF radio is now so reliable and commonplace that we take it for granted. It enjoys omnidirectional TX/RX and its 25 watts/5 watts makes up for the range lost due to the lack of height of most aerials It also offers great versatility. Just as we have already advised, crews should enjoy the comparative privacy of the low 5 watts/1watt setting more often, but if you want to make sure that all the world can hear you, the system's effectiveness can be enormously improved by using a better antenna and proper maintenance of electrical connections. VHF is not perfect, but it is a long way down the perfection track.

Under your marine safety/efficiency hat, remember that when you use marine VHF to contact the shore, you are usually dealing with experienced professionals and you both speak a language which is devoid of ambiguity. These professionals in Coast Radio Stations and Coastguard watch rooms are also there twenty-four hours a day, so your request for help, or for a telephone connection, has an assured, competent recipient, as long as you are within range.

It is also true that a variety of mobile phone and satcomms factors have meant a huge drop in demand for calls via Coast Radio Stations, so the number of establishments, channels and operators is being continually slimmed and centralised. On the other hand, the service remains very reliable and both CRS and Coastguard will continue to monitor Channel 16 even when digital distress signalling (GMDSS) is fairly general (for big ships) on Channel 70. For yachts, this will be a long time coming, so VHF will remain our most effective, general purpose communicator for the foreseeable future.

The Mobile Option

A boat telephone swings between the high of efficiency and tremendous convenience and the low of dangerous failure. Its output power is roughly 16 watts of near UHF and on land, range is usually quoted as being within sixteen and twenty kilometres of the nearest 'cell' or antenna. The figures for atmospheric ducting (as described in Chapter 1) are not yet established, but range at sea is also enhanced because cellular phone engineers try to put their aerials on tall towers on high hills and headlands, so boats clear of the land get a longer line of sight, with signals unimpaired by bumpy terrain.

As mentioned in our log/diary entry, I accessed the UK network (in bad weather) over twenty miles off Portland Bill and got into the Cherbourg antenna at about thirty-five kilometres, to have a weather exchange chat with a pal ten nautical miles out of Weymouth. This established that we had a peculiar weather pattern of high winds near Cherbourg, but much less of a problem close to the English coast.

The mobfone also overcame the weakness of the Coastguard safety reporting scheme. We dutifully tell Portland MRSC that we are leaving Lyme Regis, but normally arrive in France devoid of francs, phone card and energy to go out in the rain to report our safe arrival. We have nobody in UK who would report us overdue, so the VHF safety reporting system is fragile – unless you can tie to the pontoon and immediately dial Portland to give them the news. Which is what we now do.

Unfortunately, even though cellphone companies are improving coverage at great speed and cost, the certainty of connection is by no means universal. It also suffers the constraints of several networks and the confusion of commercial rivalry – but things are getting less complicated and more co-operative.

In simple contact terms, VHF radio brings no certainty but (in season) a very high probability, whilst the cellphone has total certainty when in range, but patchy probability off-shore and – alas – is even weaker in some of the best cruising areas like Scotland and NW Ireland.

How Does It Work?

To understand this bold simplification you need to see how the mobile phone, or cellular telephone miracle, works.

As the name infers, the country is divided up into hundreds of small areas, or cells, each served by a small, mobile telephone base station with appropriate equipment and radio antenna. This, in common with the adjacent cells, is land-line linked to a mobile telephone exchange, itself plumbed into a normal BT exchange. The mobfone's incoming radio signal, when received by the cell's antenna and radio receiver, is converted to digital pulses and sent to its final telephone exchange destination, by wire, or by fibre-optic link. It is then modified to radio digitised data for re-transmission to a mobile. Each mobile exchange has the capacity to service 60,000 mobiles.

The big companies still operate an analogue TX, RX system, but this is being phased out in favour of the greater security from eavesdroppers and cloning thieves offered by digital signal processing methods and removable, personalised PIN cards. These also offer the much more versatile electronics needed to prevent other crimes (that is, using somebody else's number) and to make communication more certain, partly because digitised data is much clearer than other signals travelling either by wire, or through the air.

Every digital phone (owner) has its own unique identity in addition to its contact number. When the unit is switched on, it locks on to the strongest signal, (usually from the nearest antenna) then transmits its mobile identity over a dedicated control channel (frequency). This tells the company's main computer where the phone is currently located and adds other data about its status, for example, whether certain types of call are barred, or if it has a Messaging service. All this happens in about 350 milliseconds and also makes a voice channel available as soon as a number is dialled. Equally, all incoming calls are directed to the appropriate, local antenna. It is clever and fascinating and makes person-to-person communication very certain as long as you are within range of a cell.

The Equipment

The topic of suitable cellular equipment receives a regular airing in the popular journals dedicated to mobile communications and it is certainly not our function to guide you through the labyrinth of mobile telephones, service providers and tariffs. There are, however, a number of general principles of particular interest to boat owners and a few hidden facts which have emerged from our purchase of a mobfone specifically for use during our annual six months aboard.

If you are already using a portable telephone for business, you will have no problems in moving it onto the boat – unless you have been duped into having a car phone, which is a fixed installation, instead of the equally powerful but more versatile mobile. This apart, you will not escape the basic economics that you can either pay the high monthly rental and lower call costs preferred by the frequent, business user, or you can go for the lower fixed charge and higher per minute tariff of the low volume user. If you are lucky, you will be excused a connection charge, but the line rental is an inescapable monthly penance.

Whichever you choose, you will be legally bound to a year's contract and possibly a three-month notice of termination. My own tactics were to do all the research via mobile phone magazines and asking around to identify the best deal for my lifestyle. I then signed up during October, knowing that I would have little winter use, but if the choice was not good for my next season, I could get a better contract for the coming year. This means staying with the same company, or suffering the £50 disconnection charge, mentioned in the very small print but rarely given as a warning to newcomers, in order to seek a better deal elsewhere.

The structure is that the big companies like Cellnet, One-to-One, Orange and Vodaphone provide the system, whilst a second organisational tier, called the service providers, markets the airtime, and a third retailer sells the hardware and the contracts and also does all the negotiating. There is a vast amount of wheeling and dealing done here, with most phones being almost given away, but the cost recouped from the call charges, etc.

Changing the set-up to be able to send facsimile messages (fax) from the boat is not a technical problem. It can be achieved by purchasing a special pocket-sized computer cum personal organiser which has a built-in telephone connector (modem) and its own digital telephone attached, or you can purchase the software and a PCMCIA card to send fax via the boat's laptop computer. This will involve exchanging the mobile phone unit for one which has an RS232, computer-style cable socket. There is not much difference in the cost of doing this. Both are expensive and should be balanced against the low cost and increasing numbers of local fax bureaux.

Extra Gear For Boats

Phone electronics are very susceptible to corrosion, so a leather protective case was an early purchase to keep out salt water droplets and as a buffer against dropping. If I carry the unit in the dinghy, a plastic bag will be added.

5.1 The voltage inverter is neat and very useful.

Keeping up the power supply is not a problem. Most mobile phones come with a mains charger and ours recharges in about thirty minutes via the boat's 200 watts voltage inverter. We also have a 12v charger which either plugs into a cigar lighter fitting, or you chop off the plug to make a direct connection to the supply. The advantage of this accessory is that it comes with a fixing mount to hold the phone safe at sea. Another £20 was spent on a spare battery, but this could be replaced by a battery eliminator, which simply powers the phone from the 12v supply. I did not do this because it had no fixed mount and I like to discharge–recharge nicad batteries totally very regularly.

So far, we do not have an external antenna because most of them are dependent on the car's metal bodywork to produce the necessary ground plane effect. From amateur radio, I can appreciate the enhanced performance that a more powerful aerial connotes, but my experiments with VHF ground planes made from biscuit tins have not been encouraging. There are dedicated marine phone antennae available at prices from £15 to £75, but a recent long cruise to south-west Ireland, the Isles of Scilly and North France has proved that we do not need this extra aerial power very often.

What Is In It For Me?

As soon as you mention marine communications, 'safety and emergency' follow, parrot-like in word association auto prompt. So, we discussed telephones with an officer of Her Majesty's Coastguard.

He told us that even though a large percentage of fishing trawlers and coasters carry mobile telephones and that most Coastguard stations have a list of local boat numbers, the crews rarely answer calls when HMCG is looking for some extra eyes out at sea, or even immediate assistance for a boat in trouble. The fishermen are either switched off, or making work noise elsewhere in the boat. Some even switch off when they are well away from the land because they realise that as soon as your telephone is classified as being abroad, the caller only pays the local toll to, say, Newbury, whilst the more expensive, overseas element of the charge is borne by the mobile telephone account holder.

There is one recorded instance of a yacht losing its mast and VHF aerial and obtaining assistance by telephone, and a number of power boat people have used the system to call out the breakdown cavalry. Small sports boat skippers have been known to get lost, then to frustrate the Coastguard by asking for a position fix by phone, when a VHF call could have passed to their direction-finding equipment. It is obviously impossible to get an RDF line on a mobile telephone. Probably, the most practical use of the mobile has been by cliff walkers telephoning with details of climbers, sailboarders, etc observed to be in trouble. All phone companies have a dedicated emergency (999-style) number which can alert HMCG, but this is slower than a VHF Mayday and will not be intercepted by other seafarers. In safety terms, carry the mobile phone at sea, but VHF will always be your best bet.

Our Service Provider contract gives £7.50-worth of free calls per month and – ashore – we initially struggled to use them. Inevitably use grew with experience, so my wife used it during a moment of apprehension in a dark car park and it was useful to access our answer machine and to avoid high hotel phone rates at the Earls Court Show. Here on the boat, it makes little direct contribution to sea safety, but brings many indirect aids – weather forecasts, keeping in touch with parents and other cruising boats. When we expected to meet friends somewhere in Ireland, the *rendezvous* was more effectively accomplished by a telephone call than by constantly monitoring and calling on VHF for several days until they caught up with us. In other years, we have had to wait in a particular location for fear of missing them, but the little cell phone has improved all that.

So far, this year, the boat phone has saved us many miles of kiosk-hunting in the rain and has been an invaluable business aid. In summer, our office is on the boat and it is more efficient because of the little Nokia using all three media – voice, fax and e-mail. It has been easy to redirect what is now cynically called snail mail, to our next destination and to keep in touch with clients. We make more money by having good on-board communications and I can see it liberating a number of different types of business people to enjoy the extended periods of cruising which we met in the Mediterranean last year – architects, wholesale pharmacist, accountant, investor and several consultants, who – like us – simultaneously work and enjoy cruising their boats for six months each year, whilst also keeping in touch with professional needs back home.

Some people tend to think that everything put onto a boat must be for marine safety and efficiency, yet my main reason for boating is that it is fun. If I can get some fun out of the mobile telephone, that is a very valid reason for having it. Here in Cherbourg and earlier in rainy Brixham, the boat phone was a great convenience and gave me a lot of pleasure. If you can afford it, then I see no reason not to have it.

Mobile Phone Speak

Analogue	System in which phone radio signal is an analogy of the human voice; subject to distortion, interference and eavesdropping.
Air time provider	Organisation retailing services provided by Cellnet, Vodaphone, etc who are legally prohibited from dealing direct with the public.
Callback	A service recording your messages, relayed to you when your mobile unit is next switched on. Charged.
Class	Output powers designated by DTI. Class 2 is used by car phones and luggables (3 watts). Class 4 is for portables (0.6 watts).
Clone	A mobile phone illegally chipped with an ident belonging to another.
Digital	Latest way of transmitting speech. Voice is converted into computer codes less affected by interference and virtually impossible to clone.
DCS1800	Euro standard for mobile phone frequencies around 1800 MHz.
ETACS	Extended Total Access Communications System – the UK standard for telephone frequencies.
GSM	Global System for Mobile Communications agreed by all European/World companies.
Hand-over:	Network method for transferring communications from one cell to another. Undetectable by the user.
PCMCIA card	Fax/modem card connecting mobile phone to computer. A PCMCIA slot is now usual on all laptop computers.
Roaming	Term used for ability to use your mobile in other countries operating GSM standards.
SIM	Subscriber Identity Module – smart card carrying the owner's identity, etc.

So, What Will It Cost?

The rates for making a normal Coast Radio Station link call via VHF are very standard and well publicised. Currently they are £1.77 per minute for calls within the UK and to Southern Ireland and (strangely) Greece. There is a three-minute minimum, which also applies to calls to all other European countries, which are charged at £2.52 per minute. You need to make your billing and/or credit card charge arrangements before you sail.

On the surface, mobile phone rates appear to be cheaper whatever your tariff. My own UK mainland rate is 37p per minute with calls timed to the nearest second. They are considerably less after 2130 and on Sundays. Tolls to France and Ireland are currently 90p per minute, charged per second, but before I can use the phone abroad, I must ask to have the 'overseas bar' lifted. Some companies charge for this, but we had no problem in using this as a bargaining chip when we recently changed our air time provider. You must also add in the standing charges, rental and possibly itemised billing. During a month's cruising so far this year, I have made eighty-two calls (that is many more than my mobile norm) taking a total of 26.5 minutes. The longest was timed at 11.22 minutes and the shortest as a mere three seconds. The toll charge for the month was £30.96, reduced by my £7.50 monthly freebies on the calls made from within UK. The free allowance does not apply to calls made from overseas.

In Conclusion

Marine communications are in a state of flux, which always connotes uncertainty and progress. HMCG is already bracing itself for a swamping of bogus (albeit well intentioned) calls when GMDSS is implemented. This has already happened in other countries. Channel 16 is often a mess and gets worse as Yottie treats VHF like a local telephone. On the other hand, mobile telephone communication is following a predictable curve of 5.8 million owners, forecast to rise to 15 million by the year 2000, forcing a better service and longer range at less cost. The sea will not escape its tentacles, so we may as well get used to its benefits. The next step will be cheap and easy satcomms. Until this arrives, the prudent mariner will go belt and braces and will carry his mobile phone on the boat. Like Everest, he will find extra uses for it because it is there. That is the decorative belt. Meanwhile the trousers will continue to be mainly supported by the VHF braces. If you have both systems: flaunt them both.

Ten Tips for the Best Use of Alternative Communications

1. Do your planning with cruising in mind so that you get a phone usable in all countries. Changing at a later date always costs money.
2. Read the small print in the contract. Reject any company asking a disconnection fee, or needing more than thirty days notice to quit.
3. Get your maximum credit raised to a level higher than you expect to use, so that you can always cope with emergencies, with no fear of the line being cut off because you have gone beyond the agreed limit.
4. Never undertake to pay your monthly bill by automatic credit card deduction. You can annul a bankers order by one telephone call. Much safer!
5. Take note of off-peak period times. From Spain, for example, this reduces the tariff from £1.10 per minute to 50 per cent of that rate.
6. Be very sparing in giving out your mobile number. Remember, if you are in Spain your correspondent only pays the local part of the call, you pay the more expensive overseas element.
7. Plan what you are going to say before you dial out. Mobile phoning is expensive. Get on – talk – get off.
8. Have a spare battery and mains/12v charger.
9. Your phone will need a secure fixing place on the boat.
10. Look at the cost effectiveness and advantages of e-mail and fax against the cost of installing the appropriate PC card into a palmheld or notebook computer.

Chapter 6

Weather Analysis Instruments

Weather and boat owners enjoy a totally love–hate relationship of when it is good it is very, very good, but when it is bad it is totally bloody. Most cruiser skippers are fascinated – even besotted – by weather. If only we had a crystal ball! Then, we should not have been stranded in Cherbourg because we missed the weather window of the week and would not have been recently battered by over forty knots of wind because we left Ireland for the Isles of Scilly on an imprecise forecast.

In spite of our experience, most of us leisure sailors let optimism triumph over probability and fancy ourselves as weather experts. Why not? We go to sea for pleasure and as long as we are not stupidly insouciant, then playing weather (WX) forecasters is part of the fun.

Increasingly, electronics has a role to play in this aspect of the hobby. The useful equipment stretches from the barometer to the full-blown weather fax chart, available from a variety of sources. Before we get involved in the technicalities, let us have a look at some of the weather prognosis and recording equipment available to us.

The Electronic Barometer

The electronic barometer has long been a favourite working tool on our much-travelled motor-sailer. It is probably the simplest, oldest, most understood and most useful of all the weather-related tools. This longevity is why it is backed up by a wealth of lore derived from centuries of real observation and experience and still has a very valid place in providing informed guesses about conditions to come.

Such doggerel as

> Sharp rise after low
> Foretells another blow

can often be seen to work, which makes the barometer a basic, very useful boat accessory.

Most of us would probably like to carry a full barograph, but boat space is limited and small cruisers are not the best environment for delicate, glass-encased instruments requiring special dry paper.

The electronic barometer has no moving parts and the paper is replaced by an LCD screen showing current pressure and the tendency (for example, Rising 1016). There is also a traffic light indicator which illuminates when a change – especially a rapid change – is taking place. This makes it more useful than the traditional clock-face barometer where, unless you make frequent observations, you have no idea of the level of change seen against time.

A most useful electronic feature is the ability to step back hour by hour through the pressure gradient over the previous twenty-four hours. During a cruise, this function can be used to perceive the trend and make plans accordingly. This is an excellent way of backing up professional forecasts and 'guesstimating' where the closely spaced isobars and low pressure nubs are in relation to your current location.

If you are seriously interested, or wish to have a graphic illustration, it takes but a couple of minutes to transcribe the 24-hour readings onto squared paper. If you do this, you are matching the barograph.

Our own instrument sits unobtrusively in the corner of the wheelhouse all summer and passes its winter on a shelf beside the office desk. It is frequently consulted, but demands no favours other than a new battery a couple of times a year. It was £150 well spent.

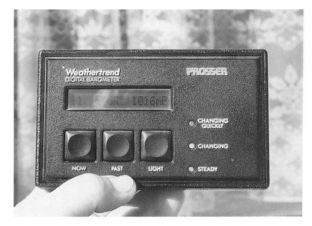

6.2 Showing the pressure an hour ago.

Navtex

Navtex has been a similar fix-it-and-forget-it accessory, but can be set up to give a wide range of weather and other useful maritime information. However, for most of us its chief function will always be the repetition of national weather forecasts, which we might have missed, plus the immediate receipt of new and cancelled gale warnings.

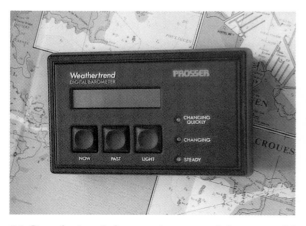

6.1 Our electronic barometer, now eight years old and still much used.

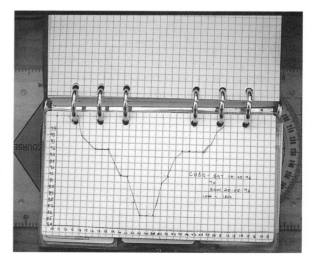

6.3 You can transcribe twenty-four hours' of information onto squared paper to make a simulated barograph reading.

An indicator of the esteem in which Navtex is now held is seen in the fact that it has been adopted as an element of the internationally supported Global Maritime Distress and Safety System (GMDSS) and is a compulsory hardware requirement on all vessels of weight 300 gross tons or more.

It is good that agreement has been reached because the early days of Navtex were soured by national pride and self-interest. Even though part of the funding was international and English was agreed as the most suitable language, some nations insisted on transmitting data in their own language first, followed by English. When this was forbidden, these countries only transmitted at erratic times and sometimes simply did not bother. Others put the task in the hands of the military, who occasionally forgot to transmit.

Before 1995, even though Navtex was by then more than ten years old, there were parts of Northern Europe and the Mediterranean where it was impossible to receive Navtex messages, even though an accessible station was shown on the coverage map. However, things are now much improved and most of the stations conceived on the Master Plan are operational and transmitting data as per their agreed schedules. This means that a boat anywhere in Europe and the Mediterranean should be within range of a main transmitter, or of one of the relay stations.

Range is governed by transmitting frequency and by such radio propagation conditions as the height of the reflecting ionospheric layer and sunspot activity. Navtex is transmitted on 518 KHz, which gives it a range of 300 nm under 'flat' conditions. This is extended by the previously mentioned relay stations.

Under some atmospheric conditions, I have frequently received Navtex signal from Niton Radio in Corsica and the Balearics. This is why each station in a defined area broadcasts at its own allotted time, otherwise a forecast from Meteo France (Toulouse) might be blotted out by Brest, or by Tarifa in Spain. Such chaos is also reduced by giving each station a designated letter and most receivers can be user-configured to receive only the desired local stations.

This selectivity is also extended to the type of message received. If you take them all, you will get gale warnings, navigational warnings, ice-flow messages, Mayday repeats, systems status messages, electronic navigation system faults and errors and a regular list of messages sent out over the past few days. Fortunately, you can program out the data which is not required. Without this facility, a video screen Navtex would be permanently cluttered with useless messages and the paper printer models would be forever chattering and spewing out paper.

You can now also set the machine to respond to such divergences as will enable you to receive UK-originated forecasts via the Dutch transmitter at Ostend when you are cruising the North Sea and there is a similar facility tuned to Niton Radio broadcasting French-supplied weather data, which is relevant to boats navigating in North France and feeling that they are well towards the outer edge of the zones covered by British met men.

The beauty of Navtex is its simplicity. You do not have to tune it, or to remember to switch it on. It automatically receives what it has been programmed to record. Equally, there is not much practical difference between models which record messages onto a video screen and those which use a roll of paper. The former is quieter, but there are advantages to having a printed message arrive.

Running costs are negligible. We are normally on our own boat for about six months a year. The Navtex is switched on in April and switched off in late September. It draws only a few milliamps and we generally go through just two rolls of paper in that time.

Most receivers will work well enough with no aerial other than the coil of thin wire supplied at purchase. If, however, you plan to cruise towards the fringes of the coverage zones, a bit of aerial assistance might be advised.

Our own solution has been to strip back about 10 cm of the antenna cable's insulation and to tape this to one of the mizzen mast backstays. All passive aerials receive better by having more wire, no matter where it runs. This simple procedure has noticeably improved reception in poor areas. The alternative is to fit a commercial active antenna, which gives more wire in the form of a coil, or comprises a small vertical rod sending a stronger signal to the receiver via a solid state pre-amplifier mounted at its base.

In theory, you can purchase the software to obtain Navtex broadcasts via any suitable single side band (SSB) receiver and a laptop computer. In practice, this is so clumsy and such a mess of cables, timers and delicate screens, that it is scarcely worth considering. For its price and size, a standard, dedicated Navtex is very fair value for money and a very useful on-board tool.

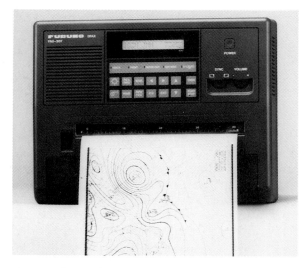

6.4 Dedicated weatherfax – expensive but superior.

On-board Weatherfax

An on-board weatherfax is a more powerful seagoing tool and can be obtained from a variety of sources. Power inevitably implies more costly equipment and a greater degree of operator involvement and skills.

The principal on-line third party information provider is Marinecall, a branch of the Met Office whose UK telephone forecasts are known to most seafarers and have been well documented in many journals. However, less well known is their fax system.

Metfax

Metfax, the facsimile transmission service, increasingly becomes part of our UK cruising armoury, both when we are dithering about leaving a British port in unsettled weather, or when we are discussing the strategy for a coastal cruise lasting several days. We invariably consult it if we are planning a Channel crossing, or any other off-shore passage. For a couple of pounds, the information is good value and might either save you from setting out into the teeth of a gale, or might persuade you to stay at home, instead of driving down to the boat for the weekend.

The range of services offered changes from time to time, but the basics are very constant. Of most interest to leisure sailors are the following.

24-hour Printed Shipping Forecast

The 24-hour printed shipping forecast is a printed version of the broadcast shipping forecast, but also gives inshore details, the general situation and an outlook for the day following the shipping forecast normal 24-hour period. It is accompanied by a chart showing pressure zones and isobars for the same two periods, that is, current day and next day. For the weekend cruiser, this is very helpful and very adequate as a planning aid.

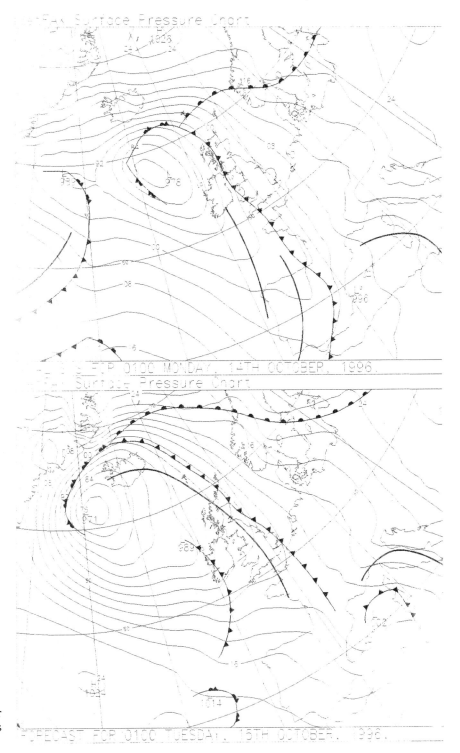

6.5 Facsimile WX chart for planning. Three pounds well spent.

4-day Forecast Charts

The 4-day forecast charts of four charts on one page looks beyond this period and is aimed at skippers venturing a bit further afield or staying out for a full week. As I write, I have taken a written forecast and chart for today (Monday) and tomorrow (Tuesday). Then separately, I have been faxed the pressure forecast charts, isobars, etc for the period Wednesday to Saturday inclusive. Nobody pretends that this is going to be very detailed, or that it is totally reliable (weather forecasting is as much a black art as an exact science) but it does give pointers. If I am planning a voyage from the South Coast over to Ireland, or going north to the Baltic, or down beyond Ushant into Biscay, I at least get an idea of whether I can expect strong or light winds and whether they will assist or hinder my progress.

The Mobile Telephone

The mobile telephone increasingly becomes part of normal cruising equipment and many of us now utilise GSM, or other digital systems, to transmit and receive data, which includes facsimile transmissions. Obtaining the latest 'official' forecasts is now easier and occasionally very valuable. Before you set off, you need to check that the forecasts for your chosen area are available by mobfone. You may have to deposit a credit sum and have the cost of each forecast deducted as you receive it.

There are a number of necessities and options, of which the most obvious is a GSM mobile telephone with an output either to a laptop computer via a PCMCIA card fitted into a slot, or to purchase a special, dedicated personal organiser, which works fine for text, but the small screen struggles with charts. Once you have the desired information saved to the computer, arranging a print-out is not much of a technical problem.

Self-generated WX Fax

A self-generated WX fax is another option and one which opens up a fascinating part of radio. There are about ninety national weather stations, scattered throughout the world, which send out a continuous stream of current weather and prognosis information. This is concerned not only with atmospheric pressures, but also has charts forecasting actual wind direction and strength, plus anticipated sea state, water temperatures and much besides. As with Navtex, the boat skipper can set up his equipment to capture, or to ignore, according to needs.

The equipment for this aspect of our hobby is not cheap, but once you have it installed, you get all the latest weather information as it is needed and free of charge.

There are two basic configurations enabling on-board capture of all this fascinating data. They are:

1. SSB radio – commercial demodulator – printer (computer could be optional).

2. SSB radio – demodulator – computer software – laptop PC – printer (optional).

The former is the simpler option and the second a little more powerful and versatile. It also requires a few more cables and greater operator technique.

The SSB Radio

The SSB radio can be one from a number used for normal marine operation, a dedicated amateur bands set, a communications receiver or even something like one of the little Sony or Grundig models. The requirement is that it shall cover the frequency range from about 30 KHz to about 30 MHz. This is the normal spread and gives access to most of the world's entertainment slots, much commercial radio and teleprinter traffic, the radio amateur bands and weather facsimile broadcasts.

Before signing a cheque, the newcomer should ascertain that the receiver has the following:

1. An external antenna socket.
2. An external audio speaker outlet.
3. The ability to receive upper side band (USB) and lower side band (LSB) on all its frequency bands.
4. The facility to tune in 1 KHz steps, or even less.

The features are standard to some marine SSB and amateur transceivers and will be found in all the, so-called, communications receivers aimed at the serious hobbyists who

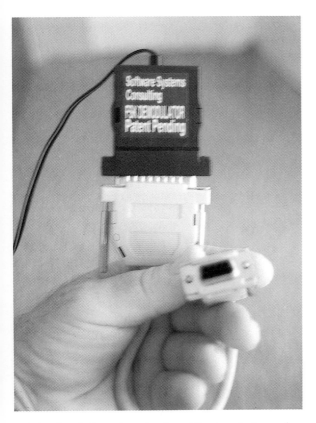

6.6 Author's ham bands rig with signal demodulator and WX fax software.

have no wish to transmit, but who derive their pleasure from listening.

The *caveat emptor* area is that of mass produced radios intended for high portability and wider entertainment. Such trade descriptions as 'worldwide' and 'total scanner' can be ignored. Without the performance features mentioned, the radio will not work as a weather tool. Price is quite a good guide. A weather-friendly SSB rig is not cheap, but can be versatile.

A good ham bands radio, for example, will cover SSB, AM and FM, so can be used for news and music, in addition to its more specialised functions.

The more sophisticated your radio, the better your weather charts will be. Good rigs have the facility to stay in the right frequency spot, but also to shift away any over-lapping, interfering stations. Many also incorporate filters, which access only the 'spot' frequency and so eliminate much of the 'noise' which gives charts too many black areas and thick isobaric lines.

The better the antenna, the better the reception, as we have already discussed.

The loudspeaker socket, or antenna take-off, is the output for all weather fax charting. Getting connected is not more difficult than plugging the chosen demodulator into the correct socket.

A good tip here is to invest in a double phono adapter. Until you have been doing it for a while, weather fax transmissions are quite difficult to tune in properly. You can watch the S-meter for best signal strength. Better still is also to listen on a pair of ordinary 'Walkman' earphones. Many stations transmit an ident in Morse, or they send out a carrier whistle which can be tuned to its null. Before the 'meat' of the transmission begins, there is also a high-pitched 'access tone', which makes a good tuning yardstick. The actual facsimile broadcast makes a noise like somebody perpetually scrunching up greaseproof paper. It is a very distinctive sound. Once heard, it is never forgotten and adjusting the tuning knob for greatest, sharp clarity is still the best way of getting perfect reception.

The Commercial Demodulator

The commercial demodulator (or signal converter) is delightfully easy to use. Once your radio is properly tuned to the correct frequency, the process is automatic. Left on receive, a radio draws very little current. The demodulator does not switch on until it recognises the start signal and then, in turn, opens up the (optional) computer, or sends signals down to the printer. The model in the illustration works particularly well because it is frequency-agile, that is, it will track the best part of the incoming signal, even if it drifts a bit because of atmospheric conditions, or some other factor affecting the signal's phasing.

If your radio has a timer, so much the better. The whole ensemble can then be left on stand-by and will take care of itself, with negligible effect on ship's battery performance.

Printer

The printer need not be anything very sophisticated. There are no colours involved other than black and white and no need for changes of fonts, densities, etc. Ink jet and bubble-jet printers are now so reliable that they are ideal for boat use, not only for WX information, but also for other tasks. Price tags below £200 are also an attraction.

Route Two

Route two is to hand your signals over to a (laptop) computer equipped with a suitable software program. The link between the two machines is again via the loudspeaker socket and a simple demodulator circuit, which comes with the software, but anybody competent with a soldering iron and a few components could also make up a reserve, or second, computer version.

PC Weatherfax for HF Radio

PC weatherfax for HF radio is a generic name covering a number of software programs all performing roughly the same function. The daddy of them all is, arguably, the series

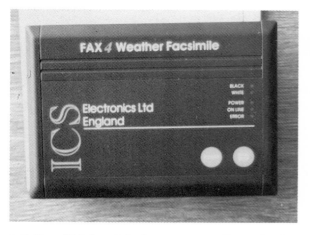

6.7 Our ICS fax 4 is frequency-agile and also covers Navtex. No computer is required. The chart is drawn straight to a lightweight, robust, bubblejet printer.

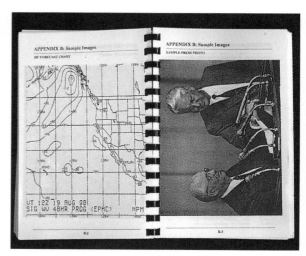

6.8 The Hoot manual is very simple to follow.

produced by US radio ham John E. Hoot. It has been selling and improving very well for about ten years and I, for instance, am currently using Version 7.0 of the software, the identification tapes and the excellent User's Manual.

Conjuring your own WX fax 'out of thin air' is a totally fascinating winter pastime for yachtsmen and a lot of fun and help in summer when you are afloat. The equipment is as described above, with the addition of any IBM compatible computer.

The beginner gets plenty of help from a couple of cassette tapes, which teach you to identify what the transmitting station is doing. There are separate noises made by the station-identification message, the warning tone, the start bleep, etc.

Hoot also guides you through the many types of WX fax on offer, gives plenty of examples of each and provides many hints on improving reception. The computer program software also does an excellent job of 'cleaning up' the on-screen image for better clarity and of correcting misalignment, improving contrast, etc.

However, be warned. Once you start to dabble with WX fax you are in a world fascinating enough to become very time-consuming, especially as the same program enables you to capture other news, agency and general visual data being sent out as broadcast, or as point-to-point transmission. The Hoot manual lists all the world's WX fax stations, plus their times on air, frequencies and chart type.

Typical entries read:

STATION GMT CHART F1 F2 F3 F4
B\RACKNELL 2:48 24 HR SIG WX
PROG 2.6185 4.7820 9.2030 14.360 3:05
24 HR UPPER AIR PROG 24 HR SIG
WX PROG 3:41 SURFACE ANALYSIS
8:06 48/72 HR SURFACE PROG
9:35 24 HR SEA STATE PROG
10:10 24 HR SEA SWELL PROG

NORTHWOOD 3:00 SCHEDULE
2.3740 3.6520 4.3070 8.3420 3:40 SIG
WIND & WX
8:00 GALE SUMMARY
18:00 SURFACE ANALYSIS
PROG = PROGNOSIS

This is a very small snippet from two of the ninety stations and I have only quoted a small selection of the charts transmitted. There is further data on ice movement, freezing zones, wind at various altitudes, radio propagation/reception probabilities, satellite imagery, sea temperatures and so on. Equally, I have only transcribed a random selection of times. Most of the stations are sending out something for every minute of every day.

The Klingenfuss Guide

The Klingenfuss Guide To Facsimile Stations is now approaching its fifteenth edition and is annually updated. It is the amateur and professional weather and facsimile 'ear-wigger's' bible. It comprises about 330 pages of how to monitor the so-called utility stations and where on the dial and when to find them. In addition to these lists, there are many pages of good reading and dozens of examples of the charts you can conjure from the ether.

Klingenfuss boasts:

- 380 frequencies
- 228 callsigns
- 93 press and meteo stations
- New fax equipment regulations
- Meteorological satellites
- 240 sample charts and the interpretation.

Klingenfuss is advertised in all radio magazines, or details are available from the publisher's office at Hagenloher Str 14, D-7400 Tuebingen, Germany.

Satellite Weather

Satellite weather images are also within the compass of the really dedicated on-board meteorologist. There is software available, but it needs more specialised equipment and is only really successful when coupled to a dedicated, dish aerial. The alternative is an ICS decoder, but this adds several hundred pounds to a yacht's bill.

Morse Code

Morse code is still used for the transmission of marine WX forecasts. This mode has great penetrative powers when propagation is poor, or when your yacht is surrounded by a marina full of radio deflecting and attenuating masts and subject to the noise of nearby thermostats and 3-phase electricity.

Class A radio amateurs must be able to read Morse at 12 wpm and this is plenty fast enough for most reception. In the Mediterranean, as an example, some of the most reliable forecasts come from Meteo France in Toulouse, or from Rome, which sends in Italian and then in English.

Hardware Problems

The problem with the hardware involved is that you need somewhere to put it all and to be able to feed it with electrical power. If your installation means that you have to clear the computer and radio away in order to lay the table for a meal, you will probably not use it too often. There is always the problem of cables being draped around the place and the present generation of computer is not really robust enough to risk out on the table, when the boat is underway – unless it is very calm, which is when you are least bothered about getting a forecast. This is not to decry DIY WX forecasting and gathering systems, but be aware that they do have their physical limitations once applied to smallish boats.

Interpretation Problems

The problem of interpretation is where the mariner's personal foibles begin to come to the surface. The cynic will maintain that because it takes a national authority about three years of full-time study to train a meteorologist (and they still get it wrong with alarming frequency), what chance is there for the amateur, armed with less powerful equipment and a user's manual?

In our own experience, an amateur expert (in a complimentary sense) gave us a forecast of NE 2.3 for our SW journey from Mallorca to Ibiza, followed by flat calm for two or three days. In the event, we got thirty-plus knots of SW headwind for about a week.

Equally, about three months ago, we left Southern Ireland on the 150-mile passage to the Isles of Scilly with half a dozen professional forecasts promising NE to E force 3–4 possibly backing S for the last couple of hours before arrival. When still seventy miles and fourteen hours from our destination, we were battening everything down and hove-to, head to big waves in over forty knots of wind which lasted for several hours.

Against this background, the amateur radio receptionist cum forecaster cannot hope to interpret pressure gradients into exact Beaufort Scale and direction. His sights must be set lower. It is probable that if we had been in possession of a WX fax chart, we would have been conversant with a wider picture than that given by verbal forecasts. We might have seen the very disturbed pattern of the weather and been able to guess that there was trouble brewing well to the south and east and south-west of the Celtic Sea. It is likely that we should not have set off into the teeth of such possible inclementness and that would have been the correct decision.

On the other hand, we must not lose sight of the fact that we go to sea for fun and that trying to match the prognosis experts is little different from our emulation of other maritime professionals. We might not match them entirely, but we do manage to get quite close.

In this, the amateur radio practitioner who bothers to learn the equipment properly and who is serious enough to study the subject in correlation to his own experience has available to him most of the data passed to the media men. In most cases it will have come from the same source. Because he can also see the local conditions around him, our yacht skipper can get very close to the paid performer. After all, he too is only offering an informed interpretation of changing facts.

Chapter 7

The Boat Radar

Boat radar increasingly descends from Dreamland to reality as usable rigs come down in size and price, and availability goes up in user-friendliness. To be able to see in the dark and to have vision penetrating the fog is now possible for small boats but – buyer beware – once you have done a cruise on a radar-equipped boat, you feel naked without it. Why?

In theory, radar can have a dozen uses, but the most important are collision avoidance and navigation. Simplistically, the radar tells you that you are not about to be run down by a freighter and that you are 035 relative and 2.9 miles off the Fairway Buoy.

The salesman rarely talks practical use, but will bamboozle you with a rapid, button-pushing shorthand list of functions EBL, VRM, SHM, CPA, interference rejection, target intensifier, off-centre setting, North-up, zoom, variable pulse width – just for starters. He tells you everything except what you really want to know. 'What will it do for me in leisure boat terms?' and 'How much will it cost, including the extras and installation?'

Price has continued to be quite good news for several years now, because radar has not kept its deluxe distance ahead of average income. At the lowest entry level of about £1,000, it is now an affordable item for many boat owners, especially as some manufacturers have developed products specifically for the shallower pocket and the less frequent user.

The choice is between the smaller, less costly Liquid Crystal Display (LCD) and the larger, Cathode Ray Tube (CRT) or raster scan sets using display technology which slightly resembles television. In totally honest terms, there is no contest between the types. If you have the space and the cash, the good big 'un will always beat the good little 'un, but let us firstly understand those factors which make radar work and why some of them are much more expensive than others.

How Radar Works

The principles of radar are historically well known and well documented and are no longer listed as one of the black arts understood only by boffins and available to nobody but the military. The name radar itself is an acronym denoting Radio Detection And Ranging. Closer analysis of these letters, which are now part of every language in the world, shows that it explains

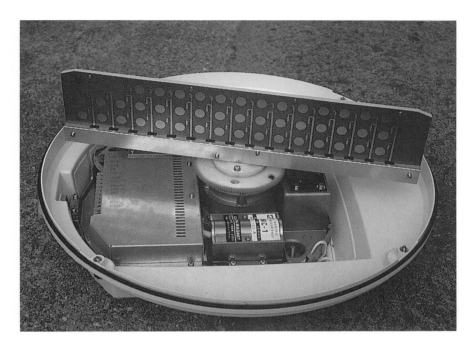

7.1 Pulses are amplified by the magnetron and transmitted by a spinning array inside the radome.

very concisely what the system does, especially in the more limited context of yacht and inshore commercial usage.

A mixture of high-power electrical and magnetic energy is fired from a magnetron gun via the scanner, or the rotating, open, antenna array in such a manner that it reflects, or rebounds from solid objects, to be received again by a different segment of the antenna. This radio-style signal is then reconverted to varying electrical impulses and passed by the feeder cable to the display unit.

There, another gun sprays a stream of electrons on to the fluorescent inside-surface of the screen to create an image. This picture-making device is called a cathode ray tube (CRT) and is very similar to television technology.

A good idea of the basic radar principle can be seen from describing it like a person shouting towards a quarry face and listening to the echo. The sound waves going out are very strong and from a precisely located source, but those coming back are weaker and it is sometimes difficult to perceive

exactly where they are coming from. Thus the antenna needs some sophisticated frequency changing and amplification circuitry to create an echo large enough for accuracy and a receptor which can determine precisely the angle of reception.

Like sound waves, the speed of radio waves is easy to measure, so timing the out and back trip gives the distance of the echo point or target as the data below show.

In one second, an electro-magnetic wave travels 300 metres (328 yards). So, a pulse making the out and back journey between scanner and target in 1 microsecond indicates that the target is 150 metres away. Another interpretation is that if a pulse takes 12.3 seconds to paint a target and return, the object is at a distance of one nautical mile.

Because the antenna is spinning through 360 degrees, it is also possible to measure the bearing of the item of interest, but this is where a bit more care needs to taken. Defining precise bearing from the boat is the more difficult of the two operations, so it must be remembered that a yacht radar will

Antenna length and beam width		
Effective length of antenna		horizontal beam width
ft	metres	degrees
3	0.9	2.5
5	1.5	1.5
7	2.1	1.0
8	2.4	0.9
12	3.6	0.6

be very exact about range, but will be less accurate about bearing.

The reason for this is the width of the transmitted beam, which is discussed in detail during the examination of specifications and their meaning (above), but for now it suffices to know that there are two measurements involved – vertical and horizontal.

Yachtsmen are not normally concerned with the vertical, except to know that it is

about 25 degrees, which is enough to keep the target in view when the boat is pitching, or when a power craft is standing on its tail before getting onto the plane.

Horizontal beam width is important enough to merit its own section of this chapter, but before we get there, have a look around your local harbour and note the different sizes of radar aerials. Even here, bigger is always better, so the longer the spinning arm, or the bigger the enclosed radome, the more powerful the beast beneath and the narrower its beam width will be.

In the early days of yacht radar, making a

7.2 The basic choice . . . the LCD . . . or

7.3 The bulkier but more powerful CRT.

selection was not a problem. There were only a couple of suitable makes and they worked on the same principle and involved looking into a tube which served to darken the surroundings in order to create enough contrast for the screen image to be discernible. This display system has been almost universally replaced by raster scan, or daylight viewing, screens of excellent contrast, acuity and video. This praise applies to both the newer LCD displays and the more 'professional' CRT models.

LCD Radar

An LCD radar display is not new, but the early versions had a deserved poor reputation. The biggest deterrent to popularity was the mediocre screen contrast coupled with the less than perfect reliability of that generation of chip technology. Each display pixel (that is, the dots making up the picture) was a bit like a computer chip and the failure of just a couple, out of the several hundred making up the screen, could create dangerous blank holes in the display. Just a few hundred pixels is not enough so – in comparison with modern LCD displays, these early radars were low on pixel count and high on that notchiness which ruins sharply-focused images.

The present generation of LCD displays is vastly improved and is so increasingly reliable that such flat screen technology undoubtedly reflects future progress. Manufacturers have generally gone a long way to solving the problem of screen degradation in bright sunlight, but LCD displays remain comparatively low in image contrast and are still relatively more difficult to read in some lights than their higher-powered CRT cousins.

On the credit side, they are small, light, robust, waterproof, economic on amps, a real boon to the smaller yacht and cheaper than their traditional counterparts. These last two factors are linked. High radar power always costs money.

In summary, the LCD radar has been aimed at the particular market of people requiring a lower cost, less powerful, smaller unit, albeit recognisably devoid of sophistication. If you simply want a radar to keep you clear of big metal ships (and plastic yachts when they are close) plus giving basic distance off and tolerable directional navigation, the LCD radar is perfectly adequate.

The LCD buyer currently has a choice between a monochrome display, which is green, or black on grey. This is dictated by the manufacturer, but we all have different sorts of eyesight and handle colours differently. In any event, it pays to see both colour schemes and to choose the one which you find easiest to read. This is as important as the specification.

Some LCD radars have the full NMEA software, which enables them to display navigational and other information on the screen. This, again, is a matter of personal choice. My own boat has most of its instrumentation visible from one position, so we have not made the interfaces. Other users do not share my preference for an uncluttered screen and obviously derive practical use from the daisy chain effect of being able to see waypoint direction as a 'lollipop' on the screen and to have boat course, speed and other data also shown, in addition to the normal radar images, rings and lines.

Perhaps the most useful feature of this is the ability to have your next waypoint on the display (generally as a lollipop with a line from the screen centre spot/ship's position) and to be able to steer straight towards it by aligning it with the ship's head marker.

Another purchase point to bear in mind is the question of 'so-called' grey imports, which are products generally bought in the Far East, or in the United States and imported into Europe. These do not come in under the banner of the national distributor and their serial numbers will not therefore appear on the distributor's records. Thus, the product is not under warranty and some agents will even refuse to repair or to service them.

Whilst researching a proposed purchase, it pays to ask about the basic construction, that is, who manufactures the 'innards', because many radars are identical machines sold under different badges and often with changed prices.

Reading the Specification and the Catalogue of Features

Power

Current LCD radars are mostly '16-milers', which means they only have enough output power to bounce a signal back from a good reflector at that range. My own radar is a 24-miler and 48 is not uncommon, but these figures are a bit misleading. From Figure 7.4, you will see that the curvature of the earth is the main limiting factor of the distance the radar can see. Again, my own antenna sits on the mizzen mast about 4.25 metres (14 feet) above sea-level, so has a limited view.

Maximum power is desirable not so much for its ability to see the quoted distance, but because it gives much stronger signal returns and much better on-screen images. A powerful radar is less likely to 'miss' a wooden or GRP yacht, a narrow target or a soft mudbank. For these reasons, public service river and estuary boats are often equipped with 48-mile radars, even though they keep them permanently on the 0.5 mile to 3-mile settings.

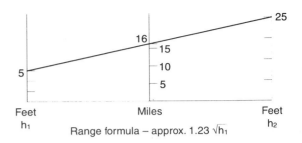

7.5 Effective range is $1.23 \sqrt{h}$ (where h = height)

Choice of Display

Raster scan display screens (sometimes called Daylight Viewing) are bulkier, marginally less robust, need more power and cost more. If you can afford the space, the battery power and the cash, they are worth every sacrifice and inconvenience. In terms of picture clarity, ease of operation, number of useful functions and the provision of safe and clear usable display, in both collision avoidance and in navigation, they out-perform LCD radars in absolutely every respect. Price apart, there is no contest.

7.6 Most radar work well. This Furuno has targeted a vessel at 4.64 nm about 28 degrees off the starboard bow.

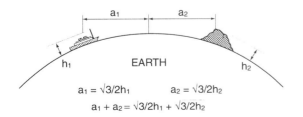

$$a_1 = \sqrt{3/2h_1} \qquad a_2 = \sqrt{3/2h_2}$$
$$a_1 + a_2 = \sqrt{3/2h_1} + \sqrt{3/2h_2}$$

7.4 Range is limited by antenna height, target height, curvature of the earth.

Cost

Cost, in fact, is now not as frightening as it used to be. The main providers are ICOM, KVH, Shipmate (Anritsu), Furuno, JRC, Marconi (Koden) and Raytheon, with the last four being the main players in the leisure market. They all make very good radars, which you can buy with confidence and there is not a great deal of price difference between them.

Good bargains can always be obtained via the major discount houses, but great care should be taken about warranty and the ease of repair and service. Does it have to go back to the supplier? How long will that take? How much will it cost to transport? Perhaps a better deal can be arranged by putting all your financial and requirement cards on the table of a local supplier and servicer and trying for an equitable deal to give him a worthwhile profit and yourself a satisfactory

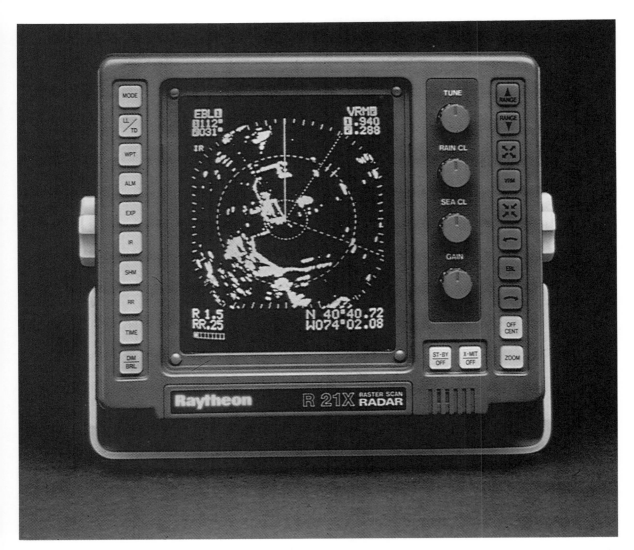

7.7 Our own radar – at this moment – would need expert interpretation.

7.8 This vessel would put a total ring of mush around the centre of a yacht radar. It is then almost unreadable.

purchase and after-sales arrangement.

A factor which confuses the price scene is the type of radar typified by the Raytheon XX series, which can be operated with the bottom-right corner of the screen working as a chart plotter, a video echo sounder, or a GPS display – as long as you have purchased the necessary extra hardware and it talks the appropriate interface language.

Not all boat buyers are enthusiastic about such an arrangement on a small screen. On very big boats, using the R40XX and up (and often with a back-up, second radar) is a super system and possibly ahead of its time. Those of us who want the radar to be a radar and nothing else, will opt for standard simplicity.

3D

The 3D approach to yacht radar is a new phenomenon in which the lower part of the screen is made into a horizontal, computer-style screen that shows targets in relation to the ship's head marker in a different way. Simplistically, it attempts to simulate the view which you would get by looking out of the forward window of a wheelhouse. Vessels which are a few degrees off the bow show up close to the vertical line (equivalent to the ship's head marker) whilst those out at 50 degrees and more, show well away from the central mark.

This is undoubtedly very clever computer technology, but needs to be considered with some care. If you put the maximum amount of information on this lower, horizontal screen, it becomes very cluttered and I have to admit that I find it difficult to read. The helicopter, 360° degree view, is much simpler. The other problem is that this secondary screen division obliterates the radar picture aft of the beam. When it is running, the radar display is not showing target vessels astern of you. If there is one incident which always worries me, it is the vessel overtaking me on a shallow angle. I have no idea whether he is slanting across me left to right, or vice versa, or even if he is dead in line. It is very difficult to know which way to turn to avoid such a monster. In theory, he should be avoiding us, but we are not always sure that he will have seen us, so we prefer to be masters of our own destiny by clearing away from under his bow. The radar plot normally shows his intentions clearly enough for us to do this, which is why I would sacrifice the astern part of my screen with very considerable reluctance.

Installation

Installation is also a consideration when making your choice, that is, how and where to install the two units involved – display and antenna.

Only you can decide how to mount your display, but – ideally – it should be where it can be seen from the steering position and preferably by more than one person. If you have the space, it is good to have the display in front of the helmsman so that ahead, left and right are the same on screen as in reality.

However, in the case of our own motor

to the crew, or to yourself ('He is 15 off the starboard bow, 3 miles') so a wide variety of mounting places is possible, without confusing the operator.

Radome or Open Array Antenna?

The marina moocher will observe two separate types of antenna, or scanner – the revolving, open array and the totally enclosed radome, which has a smaller spinning antenna revolving inside it. The former is more directionally precise and a bit more powerful, but it is also heavier and usually more expensive.

Accuracy will be discussed later, but most yacht skippers opt for the closed, radome scanner because it gives a 35 per cent reduction in both size and weight and does not have any visibly moving parts to snag on ropes and sails. The same criteria apply to powerboats and RIBs.

To ascertain what you are getting for your money, you need to understand the more esoteric terms of a radar's specification. The physical dimensions largely explain themselves and there are some engineering terms which need not concern the buyer, not only because he cannot change them, but also because they are much alike in all models. These include pulse length, noise level, noise rejection frequency, PRF, etc. Interesting if you are very technical but beyond most of us.

Most radars used in light commercial and leisure applications operate in the X Band, which is 3 cm or 9320–9500 MHz. These are sometimes called the Navigation Bands. The S band (10 cm/3000–3446) is more pertinent to longer ranges and in situations where clutter might be a problem.

Electronic Bearing Line

The electronic bearing line (EBL) is a centrally-pivoted electronic line which can be swung to lie across the target and to show its bearing relative to the boat, either on a screen edge analogue scale, or in digits on the

7.9 Our radome sits on the mizzen mast at about 5 metres above the waterline. There it is effective enough without creating too much windage well aloft. Same applies to radar reflector.

sailer we are a bit short of ideal room and found that even when dimmed, the screen diminishes forward night vision (especially through glass) and can be dangerous. We, for instance, had one very hairy exit from a narrow Mallorcan cala suddenly come a-lee. With the plotter running, I could not see out of the front window so having the radar there would have made it worse.

Luckily, our radar display is in the back corner of the wheelhouse and it was quite usable to guide us out of a potentially dangerous situation. It has been there for seven years without causing any great inconvenience. When you are plotting, irrespective of where you site the display, you either talk

How to Run a Paper Plot

Yacht radar is usually a science of approximation. The slow speed takes away the need for the quick, precise accuracy of a cargo vessel radar operator, so we can usually 'guesstimate' that a target will pass ahead or astern, without plotting its progress on paper. Sometimes, however, near enough is not good enough, so you must run a proper radar plot. Only by this can you determine another vessel's Closest Point of Approach (CPA) and when this will be. The CPA indicates just how far apart you the other vessel will be when he is at his closest point ahead, astern, or abeam. The resultant information decides whether you can maintain your present course and speed, or if you need to take avoiding action. Whenever we have a target whose bearing remains constant but his distance off is closing – irrespective of closing speed – a collision is inevitable and this can sometimes only be ascertained by a proper plot.

You can keep your paper plot on photocopied sheets of spider's webs which are the representation of a radar screen on paper. Every three minutes, the target's bearing and position (EBL and VRM) should be transferred from screen to paper look-alike. Also note the start time, or use your stopwatch. If the yacht is yawing, the helmsman should tell you by how much she is off the intended heading when you call out 'Plot'. This is added to, or subtracted from the EBL reading.

A cargo vessel doing 15 knots will have travelled 0.75 miles in 3 minutes. This will be very evident on the radar display and is enough difference to be plotted on the spider's web. Professional navigators usually plot at intervals of six minutes (1/10 of an hour) to simplify speed calculations. However, inside eight miles a three-minute plot will give you a straggly line of crosses. When you have enough of them, draw a median line down through them to show the other boat's line of travel relative your own.

Project this line beyond the centre of the plot sheet circle and drop a perpendicular to it. The length of this short line will be the closest the other vessel will come to you – as long as you both maintain present course and speed. You can also measure an approximation of the CPA time from this plot.

Professionals have velocity triangulation tables to do this, but such a simple plot is quite adequate for yacht purposes. Do some for practice on fine days with good visibility, so that you are expert when the fog comes in a busy traffic area.

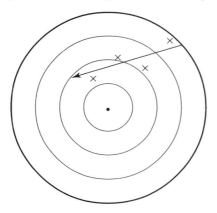

Take the median of the estimated plots

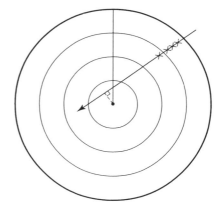

Project the plot line, drop a perpendicular to your own boat, measure the CPA

Figure 7.10

display, or both. The EBL should be set to pass right through the middle of the targeted image. For most of us, to watch another vessel's relation to the EBL is about all the plotting we need to do. If a target stays on the EBL, but his distance from you gets less, you will collide. This is no different from the hand bearing compass dictum that if the bearing of another vessel is constant, whilst the distance decreases, a collision will occur. It is, however, worth practising doing a paper plot (see information box on page 64) for times when you have several echoes which might become important. Our current radar has two EBLs, which is a very valuable feature.

Variable Range Marker

Variable range marker (VRM) is a circle concentric on the boat's position (centre of screen) and expandable to touch the front edge of any target to show its distance off. Radar can sometimes be faulted on bearing, but is always very accurate in measurement of distance and this applies to the fixed rings as well as to the variable. Our two VRMs are often in use for two ships, or one set to show how fast a tanker is closing and the other set to show that we are, say, holding position 0.65 M off the coast.

Interference Rejection

Interference rejection explains itself. When activated, it removes all the on-screen fuzz created by other radars. In areas like the Solent, a radar without this facility is almost useless and even out at sea it is worth having the IR always on.

Target Expander

The target expander enlarges the on-screen image and makes it easier to pick out from background mush. True, it makes targets seem larger than they are, but yachts are much more interested in knowing that there is something out there and where it is than in knowing its size. In practice, you soon get a 'nose' of experience which says big ship, trawler, or yacht according to the size and the quality of the image. My TE is never switched off.

Beam Width

Beam width should be visualised like the cone of light created by a torch shining through mist. It can be a very wide cone, or be shot 'up a rifle barrel' and be very narrow. In radar terms we are talking about vertical beam width – generally about 25° and so plenty wide enough to keep the target in view when the boat is pitching and rolling –

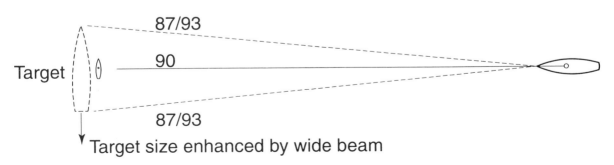

7.11 The beam begins to paint the target at 87° degrees and holds it until it passes 90°. The target appears bigger than would be the case with a narrow beam.

plus horizontal beam width. There is probably more scarist, confusing nonsense written about this latter than any other single radar topic.

Our radar energy 'cone' is created by the magnetron inside the radome and is swung round and round the boat at a speed of 24–27 revolutions per minute. Imagine that the beam width is 6° and that there is a target at 90°. The right-hand edge of the revolving cone will strike the target when the centre of the beam is on 87° and will hold it until the left hand edge passes the 93° mark.

It is true that this makes targets appear larger than they are, but does this matter for our sort of navigation? It might blend two closely spaced targets into one, but this only happens at distance, that is, in the wide part of the cone. When it comes within, say, three miles and into the narrow part of the cone, discrimination and separation are both quite adequate on all yacht radars.

I am now on my third radar. In order of age, they had beam widths of 6°, 2.5° and the 4° of the present R20X. The Koden MD3400 has 4.7 degrees and the Furuno 1830 has 4 degrees with the LCDs mostly at the 6° level.

You can get a narrower beam from an open array and warships operate on a 1° antenna whose function is to condense the power and width into penetrating narrowness.

Yachts could not handle this antenna size, nor the output current required and even if we could it would not be very useful. This is because boats roll and the on-screen image of a target (seen as a bright dot) can jump about as much as 10° either side of an EBL. A big radar mounted on the steady platform of a tanker can show direction precise to a couple of degrees, but no leisure boat radar, with wider beam and rolling platform can hope to give such fine results.

This was brought home to us on a windless, rolly evening in mid-Biscay, when *Abemama*'s radar showed a large vessel coming up astern (always the most dangerous) and obviously tracking to pass close to us. My problem was that I could not

tell on my own set which side they would pass and which way I could safely make an avoidance turn, so I called them on VHF. A very pleasant Danish lady officer of the watch replied 'I see you, but I have no intention to alter course.' What she really meant was that her steadier radar showed that she was going to slant diagonally 200 metres across our stern. Our 6° beam radar on a swinging mast was not this precise.

Transmit Power and Supply Power

Transmit power and supply power should always be listed separately. Typically, transmit power will be something like 1.5 to 3 kilowatts. This is the hugely amplified energy created by the magnetron and squirted out by the antenna. It does not mean that 3,000 watts are being pulled from your battery.

Supply power spec would typically read as 10–31vdc 33w approximately. This shows that the radar will cope with a bit of surge from either a 12v or a 24v supply and draws about 33 watts, or 2.75 amps on transmit. This is the spec for a 1.5 kw/16-mile radar (amps = watts/volts).

If you plan to use your radar for long periods, you obviously need to check the batteries. Our own machine lies dormant for 80 per cent of its life and even in use spends most of the time on low drain 'stand-by'. On long passages, we switch to transmit once every fifteen minutes and stay in this mode if there is anything within six miles of us. Even though we have massive (600 Ah) battery banks, we still run the engine one hour in five when we are sailing with all electronics on and generally motor sail at low rpm at night.

We heard the sorry tale of some of our club members who chartered an all-singing yacht for a weekend in Cherbourg, but were disappointed that the radar ran out of power after twelve hours sailing and they were also unable to start the engine. There are a number of boat management faults illustrated by this, but the most important was that they were running the radar on high power for twelve hours and the batteries would not cope. If you plan this sort of cruising, some sort of battery-charge boosting system is almost essential.

We shall deal with these in detail later but, for now, accept that a radar-equipped, pure sailing yacht needs something like the ADVERC regulator to help the batteries.

The ADVERC battery regulator with safety, a fall-back to using the alternator's own regulator if the electronic system fails, plus a circuit monitor to show how much juice your separate systems are pulling, is a very advanced way of managing and monitoring your batteries. If your boat has radar, autopilot, steaming lights and fridge, something like the ADVERC is almost indispensable in telling you when to start recharging and to ensure that you never lose the radar at a dangerous time.

Range

Range is governed by available power and varies according to manufacturer. Most radars now get down to 0.125 M or 250 yards, which means that they show all targets inside a 250 yard/metre circle.

Different models have different ratios for changing range. Our R20X has 0.125–0.25–0.75–1.5–3–6–12–24, but some larger models allow menu choice of this, or 0.25–0.5–1–2–4–8–16. In practice there is nothing to choose between the two.

Gain Control

The gain control should be reset every time the range is altered on most radars. It operates like a radio volume control and adjusts the strength of the incoming video and noise, but needs to be increased for distance and decreased for best quality of targets (or echoes) close to the boat. This is one of the more difficult controls until you learn to set it for your particular model. After a couple of

trips, the adjustment is almost automatic as you rotate the knob (or press the menu button) to give the screen that very lightly speckled background, which denotes just the right amount of gain. The normal procedure is to over-modulate the control and then let the snow ease back to a few snowflakes.

Tune

Tune is now often automatic, or is indicated by a bar graph. Some radars have auto-tune, but there are also those of us who like to see what is happening and who are content to give the setting a slight 'tweak' after each change of range.

Sea Clutter

The sea clutter control diminishes the mush caused by echoes returned from breaking waves and white horses, which radar sees as solid. Effectively, it reduces the sensitivity close to the centre of the screen and needs using with enough caution not to remove small targets with poor reflectivity – for example, speedboats, pot markers, or GRP sailing boats coming head on.

Rain Clutter

Rain clutter works in similar fashion on precipitation. It also needs similar caution, but there is no substitute for plenty of experience and knob-twiddling here.

Navdata

Navdata comes into the reckoning if you plan to put GPS and/or log and sounder readings onto the radar screen. This can be useful if some instruments are not visible from the radar position, but can also lead to a very cluttered, confusing display. I have disconnected most of mine, but will reinstall the waypoint lollipop which shows waypoint position relative to boat.

A word of warning should be given about

interface languages. The standard is increasingly NMEA0183/NMEA0184, but this is no guarantee of total compatibility. Some suppliers play around with the sentence order, or omit some lines. (One sentence equals one command, like 'Display latitude'.) Before you settle on any model you plan to interface (connect to something else), ask four or five different sources about proven compatibility. One is not enough and a salesperson is often amongst the least technically well-informed.

Ship's Head Marker

Ship's head marker (SHM) is the vertical line from the ship's apparent position at the centre of the screen, vertically up. It really represents the fore and aft line of the boat. This aspect is called Head Up and is the way radar is most often used.

Sophisticated radars offer North Up, which re-orientates the radar to look like a chart with North at the top of the page, as long as you have an electronic (autopilot) compass connected. This means that the radar picture is aligned with your chart and probably with your chart plotter.

Course Up

Course up is a very sophisticated feature and leads to some confusion between itself and Head Up. It is really of most interest to sailing boats making large amounts of leeway, or being pushed sideways by a big tide. In this mode the radar is displaying your course over ground rather than the course through the water. On most passages this makes such little difference to the quality of navigation that most of us who have this feature never seem to use it.

Off Centre

Off centre is a function which shifts the boat's position to the bottom of the screen to give an enhanced forward view. This is useful when you want to have an increased distance look along a strange coastline ahead of you and to one side. Some radars also offer lateral off-centring, which is used when the skipper wants a very wide angle view off to one side.

Guard Zone

Guard zone operates in a variety of ways. The most common permits you to draw a circle at a user-selectable distance around the boat. If anything comes within this *cordon sanitaire*, an alarm sounds. An alternative lets you draw a circle around an object which is already on screen, such as a rock, and warns you when the boat moves inside this boundary. Fishermen use this function to ensure that their nets do not get entangled in foul ground close to such a hazard.

These are the main features, but there is also a possible list of zooms, auto-switch devices, dimmers and so on – some useful and others which we only activate when we are playing.

The Learning Curve

When people tell me that their radar is not living up to expectations, discussion almost always shows that their original sights were set impossibly high. Radar is not as clear as television. More often, they have not read the handbook with sufficient care in relation to Gain, Tune and adjustments for rain and sea clutter. The second factor is that they have not given themselves enough fair weather practice to be confident interpreters of the screen images.

The relative motion of your own moving vessel and several others can be confusing until you have literally 'got the picture'. On fine days you should be interpreting a target by saying 'My heading 357. I have a vessel on 085 at 3 miles. Distance is closing but his bearing is opening out. If I look to starboard, I should be able to see his port side. He will cross ahead of us.'

In the early stages of radar ownership, a

good practice method is to put the boat head to wind/tide and slow it right down. This removes one fuzz factor by making the radar a stationary set, with everything else moving relative to it. If you have a group of beginners, it would be worth investing in one of the computer simulators such as PC Maritime's Rasim computer radar tutor, which is an excellent way of getting confidence in blind navigation – and of repeatedly running your boat into Dover Harbour wall without footing the bill.

It would be possible to write a whole book about yacht radar, and electronic progress might need two books. Space does not permit a tutorial covering all the Collision Regs or the tips about which way to turn. To go out where we came in, radar does not make you immortal, but properly installed and learned it makes you less vulnerable. It adds a new and interesting activity to cruising. If you can afford it, go for it.

Ten Practical Tips for Using Your Yacht Radar

1. Tune and re-tune every time you change range.
2. Ask another vessel to give a report on how your boat looks on his radar.
3. Radars do not like to be constantly switched on and off. It reduces life expectancy. So, once on, leave it on for the whole voyage. Running for long periods on 'stand-by' does the set no harm.
4. Periodically, wash-off the scanner, or open array, with fresh water and a mild detergent. This will improve picture quality.
5. All radars like a little bit of rain and sea clutter positive gain, even when there is no rain and no sea running.
6. Most radars have a best range. Some targets will show more clearly on, say, three miles than they do on a lower setting. The best range will vary according to make and even according to model.
7. You learn all the techniques of this chapter by constant fine weather practice – which is also fun.
8. On a long passage, look for a target before nightfall and set up the radar on it, just to verify that all is working well and that the controls are correctly set.
9. If your radar has a stand-by function automatically switching onto transmit, say, every fifteen minutes, make sure that you also have an audible alarm to coincide.
10. At night, using the dimmer function will not only save current drain, but will also protect your night vision.

Chapter 8

Sounding the Depth

If there is any sensation worse than not being entirely sure of your position and – even worse – not knowing how much water you have under the keel, I can do without it. The depth sounder is an equal electronic partner in the essential boat handling trio, whose other members are the compass and a means of fixing your position.

Unfortunately, acquiring a means of measuring the keel to seabed distance is not as simple as other branches of electronics. If you really wish to plumb the depths of confusion then set out, without knowing the subject well, to buy an echo sounder, or is it a sonar? Or a fish finder? Or a digital depth display? And what about FLES and 3D? They are all different and yet all the same.

Different, because they all display depth data in separate ways. The same, because the technologies which this gaggle of depth instruments uses to gather this information are practically identical. The engineering is also very well documented and has not changed much in the last couple of decades.

At Rock Bottom

The basic principle is that a controlled electrical signal output generates a precise number (frequency) of sound (sonar) pulses per second. The transition from electrical energy to sonar rhythm is made by a device called a transducer. This is simultaneously very like a microphone and an earpiece and is used to direct the sound pulsations down so that they bounce back up off the seabed. The speed of sound in water is a constant so, if you can measure the time each pulse takes from transmit to receive, you can calculate how far it has travelled, that is, the depth.

8.1 For most cruising applications, simple digital depth information is enough – but the flashing diode is still available.

Back at the boat, the transducer reconverts this time/distance data into electrical impulses of varying voltage levels to create patterns on a display. So, we have two necessary components – transducer and display – but when we look at different sounders, we are largely looking at the same sort of 'engine', even though we usually hand over our money to acquire the equipment according to what type of display we require. This is, in turn, dictated by the requirements of such a specific purpose as angling, or simply because the design of the instrument head pleases us.

There are a number of digital and video ways to go which are discussed below.

The Simple Digital Read-out

This is most common amongst yachtsmen, who merely wish to know how much water they have beneath the keel and sometimes to appreciate how this depth is changing. This display type has almost totally replaced the flashing neon tube but, in some cases, where the operating frequency is the same, you can convert a flasher to a digi simply by connecting it to the existing transducer, which is a good illustration of how echo sounders have progressed in data presentation rather than in signal generation.

Further proof of this no progress/much progress state of affairs is well illustrated by such increasingly popular echo sounders as the Cetrek C-Net system which uses a single transducer, obviously creating only one set of returned pulsations, to create a numeric display and a simple video picture of the shape of the seabed on the same split screen. The size of both digital and video segments can be instantly varied according to the skipper's need of the moment. If he is looking for a sand hole to take the anchor, he enlarges the video function to give an actual picture of the seabed. If he is looking primarily for a particular depth contour as an aid to precise navigation, he can emphasise the digital part of the display window. This dual display is

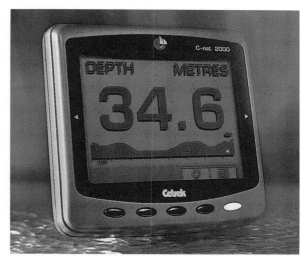

8.2 The combined digital and video display is the way of the future for cruising boats.

probably the route most yacht sounders will take in the future.

The Liquid Crystal Video Display (LCD)

This uses screen technology much akin to computer games and watch faces showing simple pictures. In the case of the echo sounder, it should, more accurately, be called a Liquid Crystal Graph, because it paints its images by varying the height of a column of small squares in direct proportion to the strength of the returned echo, which we have already mentioned. The top of the column indicates water depth and a line can be drawn across the tops of successive peaks to create a graph picture of the seabed contours – flat sand, gullies, rocks and wrecks.

The separate squares are called pixels and they can be made to light up in an infinite variety of graphic shapes. The price difference between two LCD video sounders is generally a reflection of the size and number of the screen's pixels, counted as vertical columns and horizontal lines. The greater the number, the smaller the 'dots' and the sharper the outline. Typically, on a good 76 mm x 102 mm screen of 128 x 128 pixels, a

Building up the picture

8.3 Each column of pixels represents one reading. A line across their peaks is the depth at the time.

slope will appear as a straight line. A cheaper, 'notchier' screen will show it as a staircase.

Until recently, the LCD video has been the province of the sports fisherman, but yachtsmen are increasingly taking advantage of the better information offered by improved displays and lower prices and this will be even more the case as colour LCD technology improves both in contrast and in resistance to our environment.

The Cathode Ray Tube

The cathode ray tube (CRT) is rarely seen on leisure boats in spite of its total superiority in every aspect of display and ease of interpretation. Unfortunately, it is also very bulky, sensitive to harsh environment and expensive in terms of current drain and finance.

8.4 Lowrance are justifiably famous for mono display quality. Note the solid line, the grey line and the fish.

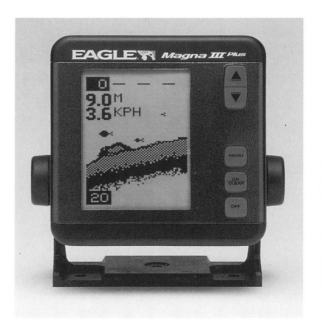

8.5 Eagle comes from the same sports fishing stable as Lowrance and both are finding favour with yachtsmen.

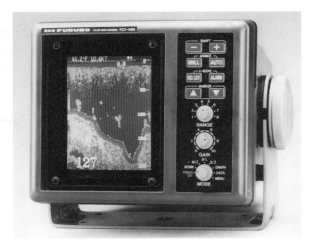

8.6 The cathode ray tube sounder is too bulky for most amateurs.

Construction

As we said, you will buy according to what sort of display 'grabs you', but you should give just as much attention to what you cannot see. Put another way, you must always buy equipment whose appearance gives you sufficient pleasure to make you use it often and so become a safe expert, but the details of the construction and operation specifications are even more important.

Output Power

Output power should be a deciding factor. Inevitably, more power means more of everything – starting with the price, but also connoting a stronger returned signal, better display contrast, better line sharpness, better ability to display small changes and to show small fish etc.

Power is specified in watts, which can be quoted as 'peak-to-peak' or in Root Mean Square (RMS) notation. Running a sounder at its full peak-to-peak setting is a bit like having a stereo speaker on full blast – mechanically there is no danger, but the distortion is so enormous that human in-terpretation of the output is impossible. RMS power (call it average power, if you like, but see the glossary of echo sounder language on page 77) should be seen as the 'usable' output/input. Some manufacturers hype up their product by quoting the peak-to-peak power, but this can be reduced to RMS by dividing by 8 when you compare like with like. (A 1600-watt peak-to-peak sounder is the same as a model offering 200 watts in the more usual RMS notation.)

Emission frequency and pulse length can be taken together for our purpose and are mostly factory-set. The basic principle is something like radio waves with lower frequencies being better for longer distances, but suffering from lessened sharpness at the user end. Commercial, deep-sea fishermen use sounders transmitting at about 50 KHz, whilst leisure boat sounders, which can usually expect a shallower water operating environment, operate at 200 KHz (or 200,000 cycles per second) with sophisticated models automatically varying the frequency to suit the water depth.

Transducer

The transducer is obviously best installed through the hull and on a faring block to hold it well clear from skin friction turbulence as the boat moves through the water. However, a reasonably powerful model will work inside the hull with only a slight loss of sensitivity. My current video sounder transducer used to be in an oil bath, then it was set into a small, sealed off, bilge space filled with a bucket of water and has now been replaced with a transducer puck shaped to the slope of the hull and secured on a bed of resin. This needs to be done carefully enough to eliminate all air bubbles. Air is the sounder's Number One enemy, followed by turbulence, which explains why the transom-mounted transducer (often operating in the disturbance of an outboard motor propeller and exhaust) is not so good and only really works well at slow speed and stop.

A puck transducer, or even a model designed for the transom, can also be bedded down onto ordinary marine silicone inside the hull. Again, be careful to eliminate air and it pays to give the bottom surface of the transducer a rub with emery cloth. The beauty of this method of installation is that the transducer can easily be moved if it is discovered not to work well at the initial location. My fishfinder sounder is currently installed in this manner and is locating fish at depths of 30 metres and more.

Some yachts are double-skinned, with either air or foam in the gap. Such hulls are not suitable for internal transducer location and even boring a hole for a through hull model needs extreme care.

The Bit Which the Eye Does Not See

Interpretation of the information displayed by the current range of LCD sounders adds a super new dimension to ordinary leisure boating and is *sine qua non* for effective fishing. To be able to do it, you need to have a mental picture of what is happening beneath the boat.

Sound Pulse Emission

The sound pulse emission radiates from the transducer similar to the beam of light from a torch and can be set narrow to create a spotlight, or wide like a floodlight. This is usually a factory prerogative, but some models have a selection menu. The area of seabed covered by the pattern varies according to this beam width angle and according to the distance to target, that is, the seabed. Simple geometry illustrates that the segment of signal at the edge of the cone travels further than the pulse at the centre (see Figure 8.7) so the receiver thinks that the 'edge' water is a bit deeper. It interprets this by showing the actual seabed as a thick (but not uniformly dense) line, especially with the strong returns in shallow water. In deep water the returned edge signal

is so weak that the problem disappears.

There are a number of misconceptions about this 'seabed' line. Echo sounder signals do not penetrate the fundus. They bounce right back whether they strike rock, metal, or silt, but the strength of return, even from the cone edge, is much increased by harder surfaces and this paints that thicker, blacker line indicating rock or wreck.

Grey Line

The grey line is sometimes part of the above confusion, which needs to be interpreted by remembering that it is not 'pure' signal, but

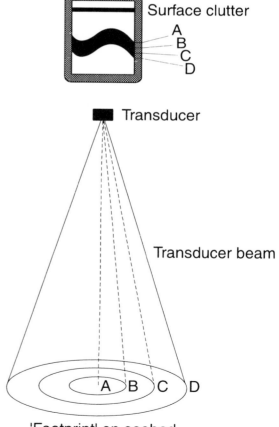

8.7 Edge echoes thicken the seabed contour line.

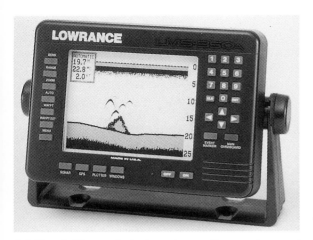

8.8 The deliberately induced grey line can be used as an interpreter.

an artificial code induced to take the fuzziness out of how the bottom surface is depicted. When signals climb above a certain strength, they are deliberately converted from black to grey, or near-white. This creates a sharper line at the actual bottom, so that small objects (especially the bottom-feeding fish which inspired the invention) stand out more clearly. Because stronger return means harder bottom a wider grey line can generally be interpreted as rock, or shale. There is no real substitute for experience here and especially that experience which comes from using a sounder where the sensitivity and the width of the grey line can be set by the user.

The skipper should equally be aware that the screen will also show any solid object which intervenes between boat and seabed, for example, fish and seaweed. Because of the 'air effect', fin fish with an air sac and also bladder wrack seaweed give particularly good signals.

What the Pennies Purchase

LCD Video Sounders

Modern LCD video sounders are currently excellent value for money, with even the cheapest offering some very sophisticated functions. There is little to choose between the mass-market suppliers – Eagle and Lowrance (from the same stable) and Humminbird. They are all American and all offer much the same features.

A simulator is invaluable. As I write, I have a good monochrome video sounder on the desk. I am able to learn its menus and functions before I go to sea and will use the simulator to find the best viewing/contrast position at installation. By having two transducers, I can switch this waterproof model (and its equally good competitors) between the console of the diving RIB and the wheelhouse of our Colvic Watson. The menus are powerful but very simple, so even inexperienced visitors to the boats can use the gear with very little instruction.

Dual Scope Transducer

A dual scope transducer is a classy device which sends out simultaneous wide (53°) beam and narrow (16°) beams coupled to a special demodulator, which compares the returned signal from each. One of its functions is to detect fish (and rocks or sand banks) away from the boat. These are shown in outline only (weaker echo) whilst the fish

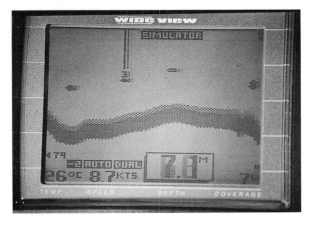

8.9 The depth of an individual fish is indicated by a vertical line.

which are directly beneath the hull are displayed as solid, black images. A further refinement is to draw a line, with digital depth also displayed, from the surface to each individual swimming lunch.

You might think that this gives the fish no chance, but Pisces has different ideas, so we can also use the sophistication for such other things as avoiding rocks when anchoring, keeping in narrow channels and locating dive wrecks more easily.

The two beams can be used simultaneously, or separately, which often raises several questions for beginners.

Where am I on the Screen?

'Where am I on the screen?' is a very common question to which the answer is 'Up in the top right-hand corner'. To verify this, remember that each returned pulse is represented by a column of pixels showing depth below the transducer at a very precise fraction of a second. This column is on the right of the screen. When the next pulse surfaces to create its vertical line of dots, Column A moves left to make room for it and then itself moves to create space for Column C. Thus, the entire picture from right-hand edge of the screen to the left as you look at it, is ground which has

already passed beneath the boat. On good sounders, this 'distance back' will be digitally displayed.

As rule of thumb, the amount of seabed covered by the beam is in direct proportion to beam angle and depth, that is, a 50 degree beam will show a circle of 50-foot diameter at 50-foot depth and so on.

Extra Functions

Extra functions are standard to all sounders.

Alarm
An alarm to activate when the depth is less than you have set is obviously useful and even more comforting if you fear that your anchor might drag towards a lee shore.

Depth Range
The depth range (to put the seabed on the bottom of the screen instead of halfway up) is normally automatic, but can be over-ridden and even set to show, say, a window of 5 metres to 10 metres if an angler suspects that his target fish are within this horizontal corridor.

Sensitivity
Sensitivity (sometimes called gain) is also usually automatic, but can be manually set to show every minute piece of seaweed and debris, or to picture only the biggest.

Zoom
A zoom does what is says it does, to magnify a portion of the floor.

Freeze
Most sounders will now freeze the scrolling image for a better look and will scroll back to the bit you missed and even save that screen to memory, so that you can trace it onto paper when you get home.

Bottom Lock
Bottom lock is a special function which takes away the ploughed field display effect of the

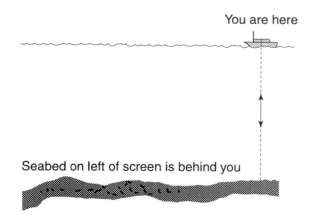

You are here

Seabed on left of screen is behind you

8.10 Q. Where am I on the screen? A. Up in the top right-hand corner

Sounder Speak

A-scope sometimes called Adscope or Fishlupe – either expands groups of returned echoes (for example, small shoal of fish) to fill major part of screen, or enlarges them in a separate screen box.

Chart speed, also called scrolling, or scroll speed. This changes the rate at which columns of pixels move across screen. It has nothing to do with boat speed. Faster chart speed equals more ground covered but less image sharpness and detail.

Dual scope another term for dual frequency.

Frequency the number of pulsations transmitted per second defined in Hertz. For example, 1 Hertz = 1 transmission per second measured peak to peak of sine wave; KHz = 1,000s of Hertz; MHz = millions of Hertz per second.

Route mean square (RMS) the square root of the average of the squares of a set of numbers. An equalising/averaging factor.

Secondary echo – a mirror image below the main contour picture, caused by pulses striking boat/surface and being reflected down/up again. Image is at twice actual depth – occasionally × 3 or even × 4 in shallow, rocky water.

Side lobe a tiny pulse segment transmitted at a shallow sideways angle. Normally fizzles out, but can cause image distortion when boat is close to a quay wall.

Surface clutter – noise distortion created by hull skin turbulence, prop bubbles, etc.

Transducer – any device which converts one form of energy into another, for example, electric to sonar.

Triducer – a device recording (usually) depth, speed and water temperature.

Window – any section of water with defined upper and lower limits.

boat rolling and shows a flat seabed as a straight line. It has several purposes, of which the most usual is estimating the height of fish, rocks and wrecks above the seabed.

Three Dimension Sounder
The three dimension sounder is still something of a mystery to many of us, in spite of its cleverness. It obtains a slightly different type of raw data via a larger dish transducer, configured to fire a very rapid burst of pulses all at slightly different angles over about 60 degrees. The returned signals are computer-processed to build up a facsimile three-dimensional image with, for example, fish shown exactly where they are in relation to the boat, gullies, etc.

This sort of sounder is more 'touchy' to install and many of us find it somewhat difficult to interpret. It is possibly more a

development for the future, but there are still other ways of getting the same 'picture'.

Forward Looking Sounder
The forward looking sounder (FLS) is much more promising. The through hull transducer looks quite normal, but has a small spur, which works similarly to an angled mirror array to transmit a stream of pulses forward and down. The latest version has a 90° beam which scans up and down to produce data processed at a mind blowing 100,000 calculations for each screen up-date. It will show rocks and wrecks ahead of the boat at a distance up to five times the water depth. Its clarity obviously depends on the hardness of the 'target' as a rebound surface, but even the new mini version can show obstructions up to 150 metres ahead. It is similar to having an underwater radar.

9.11 The 3D sounder: nearly but not quite? Unless you work at it.

'You Pays Yer Money'

In the context of the general marine trade, which is not always renowned for fairness of price structure, the electronics market is probably the most competitive and one of the best places to get a good deal. The discount house adverts are well worth scanning and can save you pounds. There are no warranty problems with sounders obtained from such suppliers and the equipment is generally very reliable. A good, versatile sounder can be anything from £150 to £1,500. In between, there is something to suit ever skipper and every boat.

Chapter 9

Choosing a Set of Boat Instruments

Boat instruments used to be an easy choice of Hobson and a few of his relations. If you had a deep pocket, you bought a whole high-tech panel from B & G or Walker, whilst we normal mortals saved the pennies for separates from Seafarer and Stowe etc. Now, however, you almost need a degree in electronics and a diploma in marketing strategies to unravel the tangle of data displays offered by at least a dozen distributors, who seem to think that we need to know everything from the phases of the moon to the temperature of each shelf in the fridge.

This is all very interesting, but also very confusing for the buyer. Some information is obviously essential to navigation, other data is fun to have, but there is also a great deal on offer which seems to have little practical purpose and often comes from designers who are long on electronic wizardry, but apparently short on seamanship. There is also the problem of too much talk of integration and interfacing, but not all instruments will talk to each other and – perhaps worst of all for us – the obfuscation of hidden-price extras. Few people even mention the dangers which can be involved by too much navigation system inter-dependence and too frequent auto control.

To avoid these perils, let us get back to simple fundamentals about what we really need to know to keep a boat safe and well, together with what is an optional extra. Also, what makes a good instrument and how much all this is going to cost us.

The basic parts of an information system are navigational and wind data, plus engine and electrical monitoring. Ideally, you should have all of them, but you might not need everything which is currently available.

An interesting pre-shopping, exercise is to sort out your 'need priorities', that is, you give absolutely essential instruments a 100 per cent mark and then estimate the others in comparison. My own list would read something like this: compass 100 per cent, oil pressure 90 per cent, engine temperature 90 per cent, depth below keel 90 per cent, a GPS navigator 85 per cent, wind speed and direction 80 per cent (even for a large power craft), charging amps 70 per cent, apparent speed 50 per cent, engine hours etc 40 per cent, circuit monitor 35 per cent and down. The priority is to buy the higher percenters first and then to add the others as I can afford them.

Alas, even this needs care, because there are cheap(ish) and simple ways of doing the shopping – or the opposite. It partly depends on which basic system your supplier is using, so by understanding the principles on which they are based, you can build up an armoury of some of the questions which need to be answered before you sign a cheque.

The Separate Ways

Most of us buy an instrument bank because we find the displays appealing. There is nothing wrong with this, but it is worth looking a bit deeper if you wish to have equipment which is totally suitable for your own style of boating and budget.

There are three principal operating systems currently on the market. They are:

1. Intelligent transducers.
2. A control/interpretation centre.
3. The halfway house between these two.

There are overlaps between these methods of gathering, interpreting and displaying data and they have a number of features in common with each other as well as with instrument sets from other manufacturers. Almost all modern equipment will 'daisy chain' its data between instruments from the same stable, but you need to be very careful when buying a mixture of displays. Some of them only 'speak' their own language, so they can pass data amongst themselves, but cannot send or receive data from, say, display heads using the ubiquitous NMEA 0183 protocol, or the newer NMEA 2000.

If your instruments are running NMEA 0183, you must ask about their ability to mix and match and to 'talk to' equipment from other manufacturers. Some manufacturers miss out an NMEA sentence which they think to be unimportant and this limits the user's choice. An esoteric language also ties you to one supplier and you are stuck with his products even if he changes the design, or goes out of business. The more other 'tools' your system can talk to, the better.

Intelligent Transducers

Do not be frightened by the name. A transducer is simply a device which transforms one form of energy into another, for example, the echo sounder transducer changes electrical pulses to sonic pulses. The intelligent transducer, as the name suggests, carries out all the interpretation of the received depth, speed, temperature, etc data by 'chips' embedded in the transducers themselves.

Some systems (Navico Corus is a current example) use a display head which has no in-built interpretive element, but is simply made up of lines and columns of pixels, which can be illuminated to show any number, letter or graphic information the designer has decided that we need. Thus, each unit can be what the user wants it to be and is changed by front panel soft keys, plus

9.1 Navico Corus – intelligent transducers and toughened glass.

dot matrix, self-label keys driving simple menus, that is, you use the same keys but with a different menu and function indicated at the foot of the screen display.

The better instruments on the market really do have some excellent physical features. For instance, the polycarbonate front with scratch resistant glass, which shows no visible sign of damage when whacked with a lump hammer. Also, by making the illumination control a dedicated button, always in the same place at the end of the row of keys, so you can invariably find it in the dark. When you are out at night, finding a torch to switch on an instrument light always seems absurd, especially if there is some danger that fumbling might cause you to push a wrong button and, for example, turn off the main navigator.

Advantages
The advantages of intelligent transducers are ease of installation, with connection by a single cable. You could also make a low-budget start with a combination digital instrument to show boat speed, depth and water temperature, then add the two analogue displays to give compass and wind. Supertwist LCD display (now common to most makes) gives a 120 times enhanced viewing arc. Above all, the intelligent transducer makes changing a broken, or outdated display head a relatively simple and low-cost project.

Disadvantages
The disadvantages of having all the work done at the sharp end are that if something does goes wrong with a totally encapsulated transducer chip, you cannot reach it to effect the repair, so the whole unit has to be replaced. Manufacturers are obviously aware of this and are 'externalising' some of their embedded eproms, or putting them in a small box inserted into the feeder cable, close to the transducer.

A Control/Interpretation Centre

There are several versions of the black box interpreter. The information gathered by standard transducers for depth, speed, compass and wind are all fed to separate sockets in a black box signal interpreter. From there, a single cable passes the entire data collection around the gang – which could also include a chart plotter.

The displays, can be a mixture of digital and analogue and have the data embedded in them. The analogue needles respond to changing voltage and the alpha numeric data lights up according to the signals sent from the black box. The speed display can only display speed and is not user/engineer configurable to show, say, position and so on.

In some light conditions, you can hold the display head at an oblique angle and will see the outlines of the possible data, even though the instrument is not switched on.

Advantages
The advantages of such a system are: (a) total ease and flexibility of installation. You can put the black box where it is dry, protected and very difficult to steal. There, it will not interfere with other equipment, or itself be affected by unscreened cables or peculiar pulses; (b) once you have the data box installed, you can add extra displays and sensors as you can afford them.

Disadvantages
The disadvantages of this popular format are: (a) it is an expensive way of buying just one instrument, that is, you must purchase all the input and output sockets for several displays, even if you plan just one multi function head; (b) most electronics work on 5 volts, so they need a 'dropper'. If that goes down at the black box, you lose the lot; (c) if the company changes the software, to add a new function, or a better display, you have to buy a complete new unit.

The Halfway House

Increasingly, we shall be offered instrument banks employing trusted, standard transducers, each feeding its own digital, or analogue, or combined display. It matters not whether the interpretive part of the system is in the display head, or is in a small capsule in the main cable. Power can be fed to any one of the displays, or individual sensor boxes and is then passed on by the daisy chain cable together with data. A combined speed/depth recorder would extract just those items from the passing NMEA signal, but a lot of other information also gets processed – sea temperature, engine hours, log distances, compass headings and navigation data all pass along the single cable until recognised and extracted by a display head.

The display screens in the illustration have no information embedded in them, so they can show an infinitely variable mixture of alpha-numeric and graphic data. This is very cleverly used in the split-screen display which shows digital depth and a simple video recording of the contours of the seabed – similar to having a separate, dedicated LCD video sounder. The versatility allows the video picture to be much larger than the digital, or vice versa as the viewer requires at the time. The picture is changed by a single button push.

Each display unit has a plug-in EPROM, or the sort of flash memory chip included in such products as the Psion Organiser, to do the actual processing of the electronic signals. The voltage is dropped by a minute 'kink in the cable' at each of the separate instruments, or by a voltage regulator in the display head itself.

The future is even more exciting, because the flash memory system means that a well-equipped yacht will be able to change the configuration of an instrument, or modify an echo sounder display to be a compass repeater, simply by plugging a laptop computer, or a personal organiser into the integral port on the back of the instrument and will then up-load the changes from a diskette supplied by the manufacturer. If the company totally changes the display style, the skipper will then not need to replace the instrument. He simply 'zaps' the software. A competent, computer-literate navigator will be able to do this himself and a marine engineer could do it in a very labour-charge saving short time.

Advantages
The advantages of the halfway house idea are: (a) the safety of being able to configure the separate heads to be whatever the engineer decides; (b) if the software is up-dated, you can get a new EPROM and plug it in yourself, or can change the flash memory, for very little cost; (c) this is also the procedure if you have a malfunction when you are a long way from company HQ, that is, a repair can arrive in a jiffy bag containing a new plug-in module, or a diskette; (d) the single cable can be on factory-fitted plugs, or on screw-down clamp fittings, so there is no limit to where you install the separate pieces, or the repeaters and the power can be fed in at any point in the cable daisy chain, or at two points

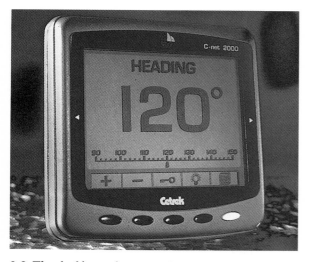

9.2 The halfway house – instruments with no embedded info, but data stored in flash eprom.

to avoid voltage-drop if you have a large instrument bank.

Disadvantages

The disadvantage is that by going for a halfway house of taking the best of the other two poles into surface mounted EPROM/flash memory technology, an instrument layout is initially a little more expensive, but becomes very competitive as your collection builds up.

Displays

A spin-off from instrument heads without embedded data, is that they make it possible to customise displays. Some racing skippers like the wind and speed to be displayed at the foot of the mast. They know that, say, 15 knots of wind abeam should give 10 knots of speed through the water, so if they are not achieving this, something needs tweaking. This requires very large digits, clearly readable back at the wheel and this can be easily introduced into non-dedicated display screens.

Digital, or Analogue, or Video?

Selecting the actual style of display can either be dictated by the manufacturer, or left to the purchaser, if there is a choice in, say, a compass head. The options are analogue, digital, dual or video.

Digital

Digital displays are very clever and capable of giving very detailed annotation, but unless the screen is of high contrast and the digits quite large, they are often not easy to read. In some instances, for example, I have to look quite hard to ascertain whether 3, 8 or 0 is being displayed. There are also many times when you do not need to know that the depth has minutely decreased from 9.87 to 9.84 metres.

Analogue

The analogue needle may not be quite as modern, but if it is not in the right place, it is immediately apparent. An oil pressure gauge, engine temperature indicator and the wind indicator are both examples where I wish to have immediate and obvious indication that a significant change has taken place. The needle shows this better than digits.

Video

Video instruments, using the sort of display common to fish-finders and sports fishing echo sounders, are increasingly being offered to yachtsmen, thanks to small screen technology developed for echo sounders. When approaching a strange harbour, or looking for a sand hole in which to drop the anchor, I get good use from the £150 video sounder fitted to the console. The Cetrek C-Net dual digi-video sounder mentioned previously does the same job and is also the way we should be asking manufacturers to go.

Dual Display Instruments

Dual display instruments are standard in several applications. The fluxgate compass is a good example where you should be able to remember the heading you intend to steer, and so are more interested in seeing that you are not deviating from it. The actual heading can be shown in a small LCD display box and any movement off-course is shown when a large, clear needle moves either port or starboard from the vertical.

Some companies like VDO carry this idea into their entire instrument range by being very strong on what they call 'instant visual recognition', that is, having an analogue needle, or a large LCD bar graph to give immediate, approximate information of the most important functions, then a much smaller screen which can be scrolled through for all the minor functions – for example, total log distances, sea water temperature, engine hours, etc.

VDO LOGIC LOG   VDO LOGIC DEPTH   VDO LOGIC LOG/DEPTH

9.3 VDO offer small analogue, but the needle gives instant visual recognition of change.

Touch Pads versus Tactile Buttons

This has been a long running war in which victory seems to be going to the latter, now that they are making them larger, springier, more durable and (more importantly) having a much greater resistance to damp air and saltwater.

I am not a fan of the desensitised touch pad, which gives no real feeling of being operated, so that when a display does not fire up, or a menu refuses to change, you have no idea whether there is a major fault, or whether you have simply not properly located and activated the pad. The lack of feel also encourages extra button pushing when a display takes a little time to warm up and the operator is not really sure that the device is switched on.

If you sail during the gloves-on winter, or go out when it is dark enough to force you to feel for switches, there is no contest between the deadness of the pad and the tangible click of the button. I also like the new kind of button which is simply 'located' in a lift-off instrument cover and can just be dropped out for cleaning, or replacement, when they show the grubbiness of use.

Switch Panels

Switch panels merit much more attention than most of us give them. I made the mistake of putting my own boat instruments on triple panel rocker switches with integral LED warning lights. At £10 a time, they were not 'give-away', but neither were they top quality – being originally designed for the car trade.

The switches do not like the marine environment and the LEDs will not stand the long hours of activity expected on boats which make off-shore passages. Of my fifteen main instrument switches, only seven LED indicators have survived two years' cruising. These encapsulated 'bulbs' are not replaceable and, now that they do not work any more, I miss their prime warning function that I have still left the engine blower running, or that the instrument bank is still active, even though I have put the covers on the displays, but I do not miss their very bright glow which detracts from good night vision when they floodlit the wheelhouse, nor am I sad to lose the unreliability of the LEDs.

The answer has been a deep financial breath and the installation of proper (over-priced?) marine switches with a painted red indicator on the on/off, rocker/toggle and a very small, circular LED indicator. This sort of switch bank is also easier to install because of the way the rear of the panel is connected on busbars.

Circuit-breakers might have been preferable to fuses but I could not afford them and fuses are simpler if you change instruments, or want to re-orientate your central panel.

Engine Monitoring Instruments

Engine monitoring instruments should be seen as a totally separate planning, purchasing and installation exercise. This is not only because they are more complex to install – and seemingly expensive for what they tell you – but choice is limited to products from far fewer manufacturers. Even though a few new imports are beginning to trickle in from America, the German giant VDO seems to have a near monopoly – not only in boats, but also in cars and aircraft.

They also make very reliable meters right across the board – oil pressure, engine hours, water/oil temperature, tacho, ammeter, voltmeter, exhaust gas temperature and fuel contents. These displays evolve without changing very much. Most of them are sensibly analogue and in conservative colours. Plenty of thought has gone into the new VDO square range, with its bayonet fixed cover and domed glass which not only gives non-glare visibility over a wider circle, but is also not the dust trap of the old, circular chrome displays. If the Perspex dome gets scratched, it lifts off for low cost replacement.

Purchase and Cost

Where to Buy Your Instruments

Within reason, it does not really matter. The modern 'daisy chain' concept makes installation very simple in electrical terms and you can often have a choice between surface mounted or 'in-dashboard' mounting. This, of course, reduces the need for the sort of professional help which can cost up to £25 an hour and means that you can buy from where is most convenient, or where they offer the best deal.

This does not preclude the local agent in favour of the discount houses. Some major manufacturers will not now supply the mail order, 'box out and forget' retailers, because they see the battle jungle of heavy discounting as disruptive to the economics and servicing of the trade as a whole. Increasingly, British adverts quote POA or Phone where there should be what you most want to know – the price.

This fudging almost always means that the advertiser is not buying direct from source, but is persuading a manufacturer's agent, or a sub-dealer, to take a much lower percentage profit for the extra sales. The question of who does the warranty work rarely arises because – plug-in EPROM and flash memory systems apart – most repairs are 'back to the factory' events to have a board replaced. This set of circumstances means that you can go direct to the dealer yourself and ask for a deal similar to what he might get when selling to a mail order company.

Whenever I write that we should all haggle, I get a stream of letters and calls from people whingeing that I am threatening their livelihood. Nonsense! Nobody is forcing them to sell to me and nobody comments that my own finances are often wrecked by the piratical prices demanded for many products as soon as they get 'marine' in their description. All successful trade is about haggling and bartering. It is great. Long may it continue.

What Will a Set of Instruments Cost?

This is more difficult to answer, because we all want different 'bridge' information. The engine apart, the basic wind, speed, depth, wind separates, or combo is pretty standard and the monthly journals are a mine of information, as well as being something of a treasure hunt to locate the best deals.

A Comprehensive Instrument Panel

This is very expensive, so could the money be better spent on something else? Even though the provision of information comes behind safety and propulsion power in the pecking order, it is also part of both these things. If you can afford it, have as much as you have space to install. The current drain is minimal and the resultant peace of mind is magical.

As mentioned in the Introduction, our own boat wheelhouse, for example, has twenty-five mechanical or electrical devices offering us information about the boat's state and progress. On night watches especially, we look at them all once every quarter of an hour. When it is dark and you are far away from land, to see all those needles and digits behaving exactly as they should, brings on a good feeling.

Chapter 10

Autopilot and Electronic Compass

Autopilots

An autopilot is another of those user-beware devices. Once you have made a long passage during which most of the steering has been done by this powerful and versatile extra crew member, you will never wish to go to sea without him. This is certainly the case during our annual pilgrimage to sunnier climes. The first leg is a 36-hour jaunt towards Camaret in West Brittany. The autopilot is engaged as soon as we clear our harbour breakwater and control is handed back to the wheel, some 36 hours later, when we are about 50 metres from our pontoon berth.

En route, all the course shifts are made from the control panel and at night we can leave the boat in the charge of Wilbur (our autopilot Third Hand) whilst we concentrate on the radar, the plot and keeping a good look-out. Next to the main compass, Wilbur is the most important accessory we have ever fitted.

Choosing an Autopilot

This is essentially a strategy of horses for courses, wherein the best model to install is dictated by a number of common factors.

1. The steering system in use.

2. The length, displacement, type and speed of the boat.

3. How much you are prepared to spend.

Before looking at these criteria in more detail, it should be pointed out that you can buy an autopilot for less than £500, or you can pay ten times this sum. Whereas a 6-metre day boat will not need a £5,000 autopilot, in general terms, the more you pay, the better the product in terms of power, versatility, quality of engineering and sophistication of electronics. This is a very fair section of the marine industry.

Type of Steering

The type of steering in use is the first autopilot (AP) criterion for choice. The most fundamental factor is whether you require a tiller pilot (TP) or a wheel pilot (WP). This latter subdivides into whether your steering is mechanical or hydraulic.

Tiller Pilots

The tiller pilot is the easiest purchase and can be installed by even the least practical skipper. It needs little more than a screwdriver, possibly a drill and the willingness to read the installation manual with care.

Autohelm were the pioneers of TPs and – as per the Hoover syndrome – many leisure sailors use the terms Autohelm (or perhaps autohelm) synonymously. The company also makes other pilots, but it is fair to recognise that they were the first really major players out on the field and their ideas have been much cloned.

The TP is basically no different from any other automatic steering system. It has all the components, which are discussed in detail further on, except that they are contained in a smaller, integral case.

Here it is appropriate to mention that our long association with the magazine trade has brought numerous calls from people seeking guidance through the electronic jungle in which to get confused and lost always means

10.1 Tiller pilots are robust but it pays to buy the most powerful you can afford.

disappointment and expense. In complaints and queries we have received regarding TPs, dissatisfaction has rarely been traced back to the product itself, but has almost always been that the skipper has tried to save a few pennies and has ended up with a TP which is too weak for the boat. It will often cope in a flat calm, but as soon as conditions worsen, which is when you most need assistance, the unit simply will not cope.

It is axiomatic that a more powerful AP, working well within its maxima, will be more efficient than a small pilot constantly being asked to generate 90 per cent of its output power. The bigger guy will last longer, will be more reliable and require less maintenance. In the long run, it will also prove to be less costly.

Wheel Pilots

The wheel pilot is only different in having the essential components as separate parts and this is generally because WPs are fitted to longer, heavier and faster hulls. They need more power. Your choice of WP will be dictated by the type of steering.

Mechanical steering

Mechanical steering can be achieved with either a bicycle-style chain around the steering wheel hub and a system of rods, or it is done by proprietary cable. Both connect the wheel to the rudder stock and will need a mechanism to attach the autopilot control panel and drive motor to the wheel hub. This is either a duplication of the chain method, running across its own sprocket at the wheel, or is a toothed belt connecting the steering wheel to the pilot's drive. The ubiquitous Autohelm WPs use this method.

The disadvantage of this purely mechanical set-up is the inherent tendency for the chain and belt connectors to stretch, or to develop some other form of minor slippage, or play. This negates the very fine, positive precision of modern electronics and can cause irritants about minor adjustment in auto-control course.

Hydraulic steering

This is a little less messy to adapt to an automatic pilot. It is a comparatively simple matter to couple the existing push-pull pumps to an electronic control system which then tells them what to do, or even to insert a separate AP pump box. Hydraulic steering should be more precise than mechanical.

Linear Drive

The Linear Drive is a third option, irrespective of type of steering and is certainly the most seaman-like, belt and braces approach to autopilotage. It is also the most expensive but, in my own opinion, it is money well spent.

The Linear Drive is a separate hydraulic pump with its own ramrod connecting straight onto the tiller quadrant – that stubby bar, or plate, sticking out from the rudder stock inside the boat. This makes it totally independent of the main steering and in the case of its failure, you could still steer the boat – and even slip it alongside a quay – entirely on the automatic system.

10.2 If possible put the Linear Drive onto the steering quadrant.

The Electronic Compass

The most important components of any AP can be deduced from the foregoing. In many cases, non-human pilotage can only control the boat's course by moving the rudder, which implies a push/pull, or a push left/push right force being fixed somewhere, together with a mechanism to tell it that the boat's head has changed direction and, therefore, needs correction. Simplistically, this is one of the previously mentioned drive units, guided by a heading sensor, or compass.

The electronic compass is now almost universally used to control the AP, even though it is possible to use a modified magnetic card sensing, via a pick-off coil, or some sort of optical link. It is not that the electronic compass can itself do anything more than the traditional device, but it does it much more quickly and the derived data can be processed to be used for other tasks.

In defining this now relatively common electronic equipment, do we mean electronic, or simply an electric compass, or the more fashionable fluxgate compass? The last is the best term, because it partly explains how the 'miracle' works.

The term fluxgate compass gives away the trade secret that it is driven by a flux element, a coil, or a toroid. In simple terms they mean much the same thing. The flux winding element is mounted on a pivot, or suspended on a plumb bob and is excited by a small electrical charge. This in turn creates a back voltage, which is at its maximum when the unit is aligned north–south along the Earth's lines of magnetic force. As the boat and compass turn east, this voltage progressively diminishes in absolute inverse proportion to the size of the angle with north – that is, the greater the angle, the lower the voltage.

Because the voltage exactly mirrors the amount of deflection from north, the unit is able to sense exactly where it is in relation to that Pole. North gives maximum voltage (Vmax), east gives a minimum signal (Vmin)

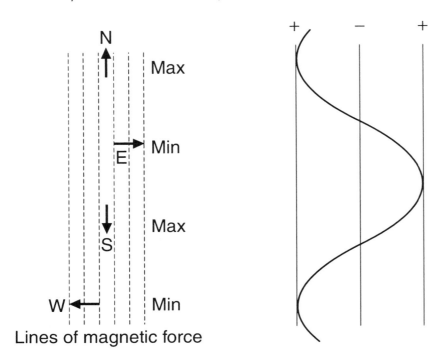

N

↑ Max

→ Min
E

↓ Max
S

W ← Min

Lines of magnetic force

+ − +

10.3 Voltage pattern varies as compass is turned.

rising again to Vmax as the turn continues to reach south.

In one complete 360-degree turn, there are obviously two Vmax and two Vmin points, which the engineers untangle by the electronics software, or by having two flux units tracking each other. This system gives the fluxgate compass a number of advantages over the magnetic card mounted in its bowl of liquid.

Speed – the Number One Advantage

It comes as a surprise to most of us to learn that the adopted industrial standard for the time a good compass takes to settle, following a rapid 360° rotation, is in excess of fifty seconds. All mariners have experienced the frustration of waiting whilst a handheld compass comes around to the bearing you plan to take, then oscillates on either side of it. Next, just as you think that you have it settled, the boat lurches and the swinging

starts again. The same phenomenon occurs when you are trying to settle the boat on a heading in waves.

With a fluxgate direction finder, this does not happen. You can spin it like a top and it still settles in a fraction of a second. When you swing the boat onto a reciprocal, or onto a new tack, the electronics track the boat's head and give a very accurate direction just as soon as the turn stops.

This makes the fluxgate compass ideal for use on fast boats, especially in waves. Honest skippers will admit that it is virtually impossible to keep a power boat within 5° (even 10° on occasions) of the intended course, especially if any sea is running.

Our own dive 'taxi' is a 7-metre rigid hull inflatable, which can be very accurately driven even in big waves when we run it on the electronic compass. It has also taken this boat across 125 miles of open water and put us directly onto our targeted French lighthouse without the aid of Decca or Satnav.

This usage alone would make it a good buy for any boat.

Split-Level Navigation

Another set of advantages is created by the fact that most fluxgate compasses are in two parts – the actual electronic black box is separate from the display. This means that you can install the more delicate module down in the bowels of the boat, where it is protected from the elements and can be sited close to the boat's centre of pitch and roll.

Such a location, with its lessened motion, would be best for any sort of compass, but for the fluxgate it is especially important. One of its weaknesses is that the sensing coil must be kept parallel to the Earth's lines of magnetic force to maintain directional accuracy. This is why it is either mounted on a pivot or suspended in space. So, the more you can protect it from excessive movement, the better it will perform.

Newcomers to electronic navigation in power boats often think that they have a faulty model because the readings go haywire when the boat is accelerated hard. They fear that the alternator is surging, or that they have an electrical fault. In fact, all that happens is that the coil pivots and swings and so trails on its suspension as the boat rapidly picks up speed. Once the boat's velocity is settled, the readings immediately return to their normal and phenomenally rapid accuracy.

This limitation, imposed by the need to keep the coil horizontal, also shows in using hand-bearing fluxgate compasses. It is disturbing to note how a few degrees lateral, or front-to-back tilt causes a major change in the read-out. Many people never master the skill of holding an electronic hand compass flat when the boat is rolling. You must balance it a bit like an experienced toper never spills his wine even when the glass is

10.4 The famous Azimuth 1000 can be either integral or have its sensor down at the centre of pitch and roll.

10.5 The Outback has automatic tilt compensation.

full and the boat rolling like a drunk. An automatic sense keeps the glass level. It can work with the compass too – and must be made to work if your sightings are to be of any real use. (The alternative is to invest in the Australian hand compass which has automatic tilt compensation.)

The two part configuration also makes life easier when you are installing the electronic compass at the steering position. Because the display unit contains no magnetic elements, it can be placed close to radio loudspeakers, radar units and electronic navigation systems without being thrown out of alignment. The sensing unit can also be made to drive any number of displays.

This lack of magnetism at the read-out makes the fluxgate compass ideal for twin-engined power boats. It is common practice to mount the compass in the centre of the console, amongst all the dials and other electrical parts. At installation, a professional compass adjuster sets the compass with compensating magnets and card realignments. If the boat develops a fault and one engine has to be shut down, the magnetic compass becomes useless – at a time when you might need it most.

Good quality fluxgates rarely need specialists to help with installation and neither do you need to go through the difficulty of anchoring the boat steady on known lines to 'swing compass' and to rectify any inaccuracies caused by other equipment in the boat.

Automatic Deviation Adjustment
Our own electronic compass – like many – has an automatic deviation program built into its software. As the boat is driven through a full 360° circle, the unit senses the amounts of lateral and of fore and aft deviation and the 'computer' automatically rectifies the compass readings to compensate for them.

This same function can also be used to put in local magnetic variation for navigators who do not like doing elementary mental arithmetic. If your boat always stays in the same area, this is probably well worth doing.

The skipper can also select from a wide range of display types when he is purchasing the fluxgate model – swinging card, digital, parallel graticule, or straight digital. Some compasses even permit you to change the display style as you go along. This can also be an essential part of using its many functions. Like most electronic navigation aids, the fluxgate compass is a very versatile tool.

How Many Functions?

We have 'top of the range' compasses fitted both to our dive boat, which will do 40 knots, and to our cruising motor-sailer, whose maximum hull speed is about 8 knots. On both vessels the multi-function screens are very useful and typical of most good units. At power-up, the unit automatically performs a self-test. If it locates a problem it will usually show its nature as a screen message. Once it has settled, a single key push enables the first function mode.

Compass Mode
Compass mode shows the direction of the boat's head as an LCD read-out in standard three-figure digital notation. A second touch augments this with an analogue display showing heading in relation to north, which is itself one of the fixed items of the display arranged around the screen. The single spike can be increased to show all the degrees from north to south.

If we are steering due east, this will be shown as 090 in digits and as a screen edge marker in the 3 o'clock position. Alternatively the entire 12 o'clock to 3 o'clock right angle segment of the screen edge display will show all 90 degrees as LCD spikes.

Off-Course Mode
Off-course mode is entered by a single key stroke. It is probably where we spend most of our running time. The digital read-out in the centre of the screen can be set to show the

direction of the boat's head. At the top of the screen, analogue spikes light up on the appropriate side of the 12 o'clock position and spread out to show the trend of any change of direction and how fast it is happening.

A second part of this function fixes the digital display on the course you have selected to steer, whilst the analogue spikes show how and by how much you are deviating from it. A one-degree error to port causes a single spike to show on the left. Two degrees means two spikes and five degrees lights the entire segment to 11 o'clock. An alarm can be set to sound when the boat becomes further off line than the skipper is prepared to tolerate.

This function is excellent on a sailing boat because it shows how much you are luffing, or are letting the bow drop off the wind. It is also a very good way of monitoring how well the autopilot is performing and assists the skipper in deciding if it needs a little more anti-yaw control, or more help for the rudder.

In fast boats, we go everywhere in off-course mode. It is a remarkably efficient way of keeping the boat on course over long distances, especially in poor visibility, or when you are too far off-shore for any land-marks to show. As long as the screen remains clear of spikes, we know that the boat is on track and that we are not steering a zigzag, over-correcting course which frequently crosses the rhumb-line – as often happens to ordinary compass watchers.

Off-Course Trend

Off-course trend is the third function which acts as a steering monitor by memorising the helmsman's temporary deviations and computing them into a general direction line. In effect it tells him that even though he is aiming to steer 090, he is a little right-hand down and is more often inclined to steer south of this heading than north. A skipper running a dead reckoning will consult this feature from time to time and use its information to make his chart plot.

Head and Lift
Head and lift are pure sail-boat functions showing the helmsman whether the wind is heading him, and so moving him onto a poor course line, or if he is being lifted onto a better line, that is, clawing more ground towards an up-wind target. The function can also be set to memorise port and starboard tacks so that the boat can be settled very quickly onto the correct heading as soon as she is brought about.

Current Trend of Head
This is really a big boat or ship facility. Some of these turn so slowly that the transverse movement of the bow is almost indiscernible to the eye. Captains get very anxious if they have ordered a course change but the ship's head appears not to be coming round against the wind – or is coming round too fast.

In this mode, direction is again shown digitally, but a screen edge gyroscope spins clockwise or anti-clockwise to show turning trend. It also speeds and slows to show the rate of turn.

10.6 Fluxgate compass with electronic spikes' showing.

Autopilot Speak

Autopilot software is an unavoidable term because the latest technology relies heavily on computer-style programmed chips and EPROMS to give, receive and interpret data from the contributing parts of the total machine. This whole is too sophisticated to be housed in the same box as the drive unit. An advantage of this separation is that any improvement in the program can be incorporated without replacing the whole.

The **data box** (sometimes known as the Distribution Box) is a clearing house for the power connections and the data-handling cables. It places the power supply cables for the drive unit where they can be switched on/off, or sent pos/neg to change direction. If the AP is sharing information with a navigator, or a log, this can also be fed into the box.

The **rudder reference** unit is an important in-put to this meeting place. Its function is to prevent the AP from making the assumption that the rudder is where is was last left. It sends out a varying voltage signal to give the rudder's actual current angle of deflection and its deflection trend.
The message is created either by a circular arm varying the voltage of a potentiometer or by sliding a steel rod in and out of an electrified coil. This is a very simple and robust way of generating the same voltage changes.

The **rudder indicator** is a feature which spins off from this. Our own AP has an in-built LCD display which puts up a graphic illustration of the rudder position. It could also be displayed on a separate instrument. Whichever way you choose, you will be glad to have it when manoeuvring any wheel-steered vessel. It is also a good indicator of how well you have the AP set up when sailing. If the boat is carrying too much weather helm, a software setting (or a sail) adjustment can be made.

Other Systems

The features described are those on our own compasses. Certain manufacturers omit some of them and most have their own particular way of displaying the information. Off-course, for instance can be shown by a swinging needle, an LCD boat upright on the screen and deviating either side of head up, or it can be indicated by red and green lights illuminating on the appropriate side and in deviation ratio. Each user will vary in preferred screens and dials and in the number of functions. There is certainly plenty of choice in both.

10.7 Standard style potentiometer rudder reference unit.

Ten Tips for Fitting and Using an Autopilot

1. Even though all turns can be made on the autopilot's course-change button, avoid using this to make very large turns. They put too much strain on all the parts which take the pressure.
2. There are some pilot display heads which can accept a wide variety of data from other instruments. If possible keep the screen clear. The autopilot's chief function is maintenance of course. Leave other interpretation to the tools designed for it.

3. Interfacing the autopilot to a navigator is a very ineffective way of controlling a sailing boat unless it is going downwind and there is no tide.

4. Interfacing a power boat pilot to a GPS also has its disadvantages and dangers. The interfaced pilot will always try to nudge the boat to the waypoint, even when it would be faster and more efficient to let the boat slant across the waves, or be angled a bit by the tide.

5. Only rarely will the ship's main magnetic compass and the autopilot fluxgate agree with each other. Check them both and then decide which one you will use to set your course.

6. Your hourly log should have a column which notes the setting on the autopilot compass, especially if this differs from the steering compass.

7. The dodge control should always be used in lobster pot country, because it always brings the boat back on track when released.

8. Get into the habit of noting the compass course every time you disengage the automatic steering. Then, when you need to do it in an emergency, you have a mental note of how to get back to your heading.

9. If your pilot has a back light, get into the habit of switching it on before darkness falls. Then you do not risk shutting the pilot off, or changing its settings, when you are fumbling around trying to locate the light switch.

10. Service the pilot regularly. On long passages it gets worked very hard. After each journey, tighten up all the nuts, bolts, connectors and pipe fittings. Check the hydraulic fluid after each passage.

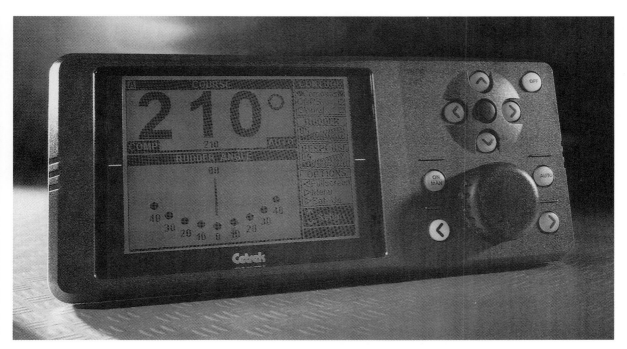

10.8 Our autopilot control head has an in-built rudder angle indicator.

Chapter 11

Chart Plotters

Visitors to our Colvic Watson motor-sailer come aboard to look at the GPS, but stay to play with the chart plotter. I understand their fascination, because even though I have navigated thousands of miles with the aid of the chart plotter's numerous electronic charts, contained in easily stored, small data cartridges, I still marvel that I can zoom out to display the whole of Europe on the screen, then zoom in to locate a specific pontoon in my local marina.

Night watches on long passages are made considerably easier and safer as Pakman (the familiar name for our GPS-driven chart plotter's flashing, position-indicating cursor) blinks his way along an electronic line, which I have drawn a month ago when I was planning the trip from Brixham to Biscay. I can see at a glance where we are and can simply transfer this position to the ship's log. If we stray from our course, this is immediately apparent. It makes life easier and safer when the boat is bucking about enough to make a paper plot difficult to perform, with a sea-tired brain.

Modern navigation is clever, exciting and very heady stuff, but it is also very safe stuff. This belief has been reinforced by a couple of happenings this year. We were heading up Bantry Bay towards Glengariff, via the northern inshore route between the mainland and the string of islands very close to the shore. As it can do so often in Southern Ireland, the visibility diminished very rapidly and very totally, so the narrow passages of the inshore route became

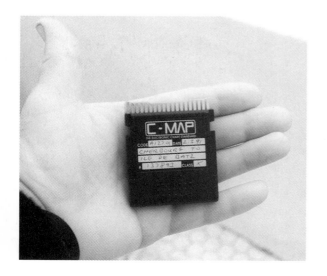

11.1 The marvel of ninety-three charts on one tiny cartridge.

the stuff that ulcers are made of.

Luckily we had the Chartnav plotter running, so had an immediate picture of where we were, accurate to about 50 metres. This showed that we could lay a course between two of the islands to starboard of our course line in order to reach deep and clear water. Translating this information into a practical, navigational form was just a matter of plonking the cursor on a safe spot on the electronic chart, which responded with the guidance that to reach it we needed to steer 110 T for 2.3 miles.

We did not need to drop the sails, or otherwise to slow the boat and were certainly not apprehensive about our position and progress. The fact that the chart plotter had counselled us to a correct decision was confirmed 90 seconds later, when the radar had warmed up and showed the pair of islands, which we would pass between, on our 110 heading. Then, even more proof was evidenced when we did a paper plot with pencil and rulers and that also agreed with the electronic cartographer's counsel.

The plotter also got us out of trouble during a 5-mile Sunday morning jaunt from Falmouth to the Helford River. The Cornish sea fog closed in with the speed of Trelawney's steed and very soon reduced the visibility to less than 50 metres. As we were very close under Pendennis Head and navigating by eyeball pilotage, we should have been anxious.

As it was, an electronic bearing from our position, as shown on the chartplotter, was easy to establish to one of the big ship channel buoys and we simply motor sailed down this line whilst we sorted ourselves out on paper and fired up the radar.

The advantages of the chart plotter in both these instances were, firstly, that we had a very clear and very immediate on-screen picture of where we were at that very moment and precise to within the 50 metres maximum radius circle error of GPS, influenced by Selective Availability, but almost certainly better than this. Ultra precision is not necessary in such cases. The important facts are speed and certainty of the position fix.

Secondly, we were able to plot our course to a safe and physically verifiable point (the navigation buoy) very quickly and very certainly. There was no likelihood of running into danger caused by the errors of panic. We had all the systems checking each other out – crew's instinct, the GPS, the paper chart plot, the electronic chart plotter and the radar. They all came together as only electronics and experience can.

What is a Chart Plotter?

So, how do we define this very powerful navigational tool? Like many things about boats there is no simple umbrella description. There are very sophisticated chart plotters with a screen as large and as coloured as a television set. There is also an emerging generation of slimmer and lighter liquid crystal display (LCD) units. Also, we must not forget that halfway house of the puck-driven plotter (Yeoman style) which uses a small, hand-manipulated screen with a conventional paper chart.

No matter which chart plotter configuration you choose, you still need the three basic components:

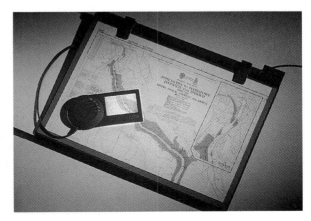

11.2 Halfway house – the puck-driven plotter.

1. An electromechanical device to interpret charts.

2. A cartographic system – paper, or more usually electronic.
3. An integrated position fixing system – GPS, Decca, Loran-C, or one of the esoteric private systems used by surveyors, or the very secret methods of the military.

For the sake of our simplicity, we shall assume that the engine is a GPS receiver, which might be built into the plotter itself, or be an external unit.

CRT or LCD?

In talking about the physical engineering of chart plotters, you cannot escape analogy with fishfinders and radar screens, where the normal choice is between the bulkier and more expensive Cathode Ray Tube (CRT) displays and the slimmer, lighter, cheaper – but much less contrasting and easy to read – LCD models. It bears repeating that more power is more expensive in terms of current drain and more expensive in terms of money. If you can support both these outgoings, the CRT plotter will out-perform its LCD cousin in almost every aspect, even though they use exactly the same digitised, encapsulated electronic charts.

The Criteria for Choice

Most of us will choose our chart plotter hardware from parameters of finance and boat space – which are often co-relative, that is, if you have plenty of money, you probably have a larger boat. Whatever your powers, it is important that you install a model which you find to be appealing to the eye and easy to use. Then you will use it more often and more efficiently. We tend to forget that we are leisure sailors, so it is important that we like the equipment we install.

We are currently at a stage in which

anybody going out to buy a chart plotter, should go in the fastest car available, because by the time you get the product down to the boat, it will probably be out of date.

Luckily, this is not too serious a problem, because the most important part of the package will be the software – the actual chart and the system by which it is interpreted to the screen. This changes less often and less confusingly than the hardware but it still contributes to a topic about which there is a great deal of confusion.

The global picture is made more complicated because commercial, big ship operators have different requirements and are more rigorously controlled than their pleasure boating fellows. Electronic cartographers and hardware producers want the prestige of supplying the big ships complying with rigorous standards for safety and quality and can charge them very high prices. These costs are beyond average boat owners, but these smaller fry represent a vast potential mass market.

Market simplicity is not only eroded by the fact that ships bound by laws concerning their charts require them to be different from acceptable yacht versions, but also because leisure chart plotters need to be small and power-efficient, whereas commercial vessels can easily operate charting devices more akin to personal computers. This has led C-MAP and Navionics (the two biggest names in electronic charting) to offer a variety of systems and styles.

If you are wise, you will be more likely to choose your chart plotter for reasons of software than because of the machine itself. These criteria are, in turn, totally decided by how the electronic chart was made by converting the original paper products into screen display images. The most important ways of converting paper charts and other information into an electronic version are Raster Scanning and Digital Vectorising.

What are colloquially known as raster charts, should more accurately be called raster scan charts. They are photographed, or photocopied, versions of existing paper charts, converted exactly as they stand and exactly as you would buy them as sheets of paper at a retail outlet. The process is executed by a huge frame camera big enough to scan lines across a chart and to convert them into digitised data. This is very similar to the way in which a document can be scanned into a computer. The data is subsequently re-converted to a screen image.

Raster charts are relatively easy to produce, but they are very difficult to modify at the production stage. If the chart contains any errors, they will also be copied. The navigator, even with the finesse of electronics, can only have on screen exactly what was on the original paper chart. This means that seamless zooming in to a large scale is not really possible. It is a weakness of raster charts that the control of zoom is only minimal and there is no facility to add more detail for close navigation, or to remove it from the screen (and back into memory) if you are finding the screen too cluttered for clarity.

The reason for this is seen in the way the photocopier works. It examines the chart, line by line and copies exactly the colour and position of thousands of pixels (dots) per square inch. This is the cheapest and simplest way of putting a paper chart into a form which can be screened. The Admiralty Raster Scan Charting Service (ARCS) is still the best example of this process, which produces really super charts – as long as you have a sufficiently powerful Personal Computer (PC) to run them, or have installed an appropriately dedicated chart plotter, utilising many computer conventions and functions. This implies a very fast computer, with plenty of RAM, a CD drive and a full 256-colour palette video board controlling the display. If you have machinery of an inferior specification, the charts are almost impossible to use.

At their best, ARCS charts are a delight to use because they are in the familiar colours, have normal identification names, numbers, etc and carry symbols with which we are all familiar. On screen, they look great and are a fine navigational tool on a vessel large enough and dry enough to carry a standard PC (or a marinised version) run on a 230v supply, but we must also recognise that raster scanning has limitations, namely that it has been overtaken by better technology.

As already mentioned, one problem is that because the whole chart must be used during the conversion process, any errors cannot be electronically corrected. The Admiralty solution has been to split each chart into smaller tiles. When a correction is needed, the small tile is scrubbed and a new one inserted. The Admiralty has an excellent system of sending out monthly corrections – a sort of Notice to Mariners – on compact disk.

In computer memory terms, raster charts are greedy, because each pixel's position has to be stored in memory – which is how the computer recognises them and their position. They cannot be called to screen by a latitude/longitude reference, which reciprocally means that they cannot be directly connected to a GPS unit and the ability to have many zoom levels is also limited.

To get over this, the method is either to insert some latitude/longitude reference points during scanning, or to overlay the chart with a latitude/longitude matrix grid, which the GPS recognises. All very clever, but raster chart users can only have what is on the original chart – nothing more and nothing less. Fortunately, in the case of the Admiralty, the basic product is – arguably – the best in the world.

Putting really precise, pin-point positions on a raster chart is also confused because of the variety of datum (start reference) points used by the various national bodies, who swap survey data with each other. The logical datum to reference latitude is the very centre of the earth, which is not a perfect sphere, so nobody can agree the centre's exact position.

This gives rise to those chart notices which typically say, 'satellite derived positions should be moved 0.03 minutes southward and 0.09 minutes eastward'. Easy to do in an office, less so in a bucking wheelhouse. This is why most GPS units let you set a chart datum to make the correction for you – if you can find out what datum the chart actually uses. My chart collection has versions using six different starter points, but some of these charts do not indicate to which datum they are written, so I do not know which GPS correction to apply. Happily progress is being made to put all charts into GPS/US/WGS84 format, which is the one favoured by raw GPS information.

We are Making Good Progress

Even the best of the early, digitised charts suffered the disadvantage that they needed to keep things simple enough to avoid screen clutter, so every point of navigational interest was shown as a small diamond. In order to obtain identification, you place the cursor over the diamond, then wait a couple of seconds until details of the buoy, or the characteristics of the light appear in a separate information box. This is a very minor criticism, but is valid because it has been partially solved by newer technology.

Digitally vectorised charts should be visualised like drawing the basic outline of the coast and rocks, then overlaying it with separate transparent, acetate sheets, each containing one cartographic element. Thus, you could simultaneously see depth contours at 5 metres, 10 metres, 20 metres and 50 metres, place names, buoys, tide races, drying heights, submarine cables, various wrecks and the nature of the seabed by having all the acetates *in situ*.

This gives a crowded picture, which can be clearly managed on a large paper chart a couple of feet across, but makes an electronic screen display almost unreadable. When weather conditions are difficult, simplicity and clarity become important.

Practical examples are that you do not

need to see wrecks at 60 metres if you are driving a yacht and might only need the 10-metre depth contour. Place names are not always needed, nor are the names of buoys.

The vector chart not only allows the user (temporarily) to strip out confusing detail, but also enables the compiler to incorporate the 200-plus chart symbols which are used by the Admiralty. My diamond can be replaced with the proper chart symbol for a port hand marker, an anchorage, a bridge, a pilot station, a chimney, a Coastguard station and so on. This gives instant visual appreciation, which is then enhanced and amplified by putting the cursor on the point of interest and waiting a couple of seconds for further information to appear in the screen's data box. This will give, say, a light's characteristics, or will show the actual name of a wreck or a buoy.

Vector charts replace the raster's camera with a computer-driven tracing system, which follows the outline of a coast, then adds in such protruding features as harbour walls and outlying rocks. The process is entirely controlled by a human operator, whose task is to check and avoid computer errors caused by automation. The compiler also gives each chart feature its own address in latitude and longitude. This, together with the appropriate symbol, is recognised by the computer reading the chart and then locating precisely on the screen. This system occupies much less precious computer memory and makes the chart a little more accurate.

The operator inserts these features with a magnifying glass device and focuses over each square of the original paper chart in order to locate them with total precision. Each has its own code for what it is (for example, North Cardinal Mark) and its details of height, colour, topmark and position. The correct cartographic symbol appears on the screen and the details can be called up from a menu, if the navigator needs them.

Raster or Vector?

This can only be answered by the Professor Joad's classic 'It all depends . . .' Both systems are excellent. Obviously, vectorised charts are more versatile, but the Admiralty ARCS (Admiralty Raster Chart Service) charts are superb in quality and have the reliability for which the Hydrographic Office is famous. They will probably always be available to leisure sailors, but the future undoubtedly really belongs to vectorised cartography.

Personal computer chart technology is developing and is here to stay. The big ship, or very large yacht chart plotter is more like a PC than a marine instrument display. Its generously-sized, high contrast, multi-coloured screen handles all the detail with ease. It therefore follows that when somebody develops a properly marinised PC at a sensible price, this will be the system of the future – even for the leisure boater.

In the commercial world, they need to have very strict rules about quality. There are already some ships operating entirely on electronic charts with a meagre paper chart back-up. They are currently using both raster and vector, but will undoubtedly opt for the latter to satisfy full ECDIS requirements.

Electronic chart display and information systems (ECDIS) is the internationally recognised charting standard. It uses only charts from such official national hydrographic agencies as the Admiralty and needs vector capabilities.

One reason for this is the technological advance which can overlay the radar display on top of a chart shown on a computer style VDU. (This system is fully described in Chapter 13.) Imagine the situation where you need to steer between two buoys marking a narrow channel, but the radar screen shows half a dozen targets in the vicinity. Some of these might be half-tide rocks currently above sea level, or they might be other vessels.

If the screen chart is very cluttered, super-imposing the radar picture onto it would neither assist interpretation nor identification. However, if you can clear the screen of all unwanted detail and just leave the main buoys showing, it would be easy to make the radar images of them sit exactly on top of the chart symbols. The navigator can then clearly see which are the two buoys and deduces that all the rest are boats, etc. By aligning his own vessel so that the radar's ship's head marker (or course line) passes between the identified buoys, the navigator can steer between them with confidence.

Seamless cartography is another term which you cannot avoid. When I move the cursor of my own (rather antiquated, five-year-old) chart plotter so that it passes beyond the edge of the map or page which I am currently using, the picture clears and there is a five second hiatus whilst the segment that the cursor has passed into is redrawn to the screen.

This minor irritant is removed by using so-called seamless cartography, which lets the cursor scroll from one chart to another without a break, in a similar manner to a computer scrolling down a document page after page. If you are travelling along a coast covered by several charts, you will not notice when the plotter passes from one to the next.

This is called horizontal scrolling and works because coastal, passage-making charts are generally drawn to the same scale and have the same amount of detail – or lack of it. Life gets more difficult when the plotter is asked to scroll vertically from a passage chart to a harbour plan of vastly different scale and amount of detail. Then, the jump and redraw still happens, or one chart or the other must be put out of kilter in what is shown.

There is also the problem of chart projection, that is, the process of representing the surface of a globe on a flat paper or screen. Mercator is the normally accepted chart projection and some understanding of how it works is still necessary for best navigation.

The Mercator projection is derived by imagining a transparent globe wrapped inside a tube of paper. The paper will touch the sphere at the Equator. If you now imagine that our hollow globe has the grid lines of latitude and longitude etched onto its surface and has a light in its centre, you see that, at the Equator, the shadow of the parallels of latitude projected onto our paper cylinder will be roughly the same distance apart as they are on our glass globe. As you travel further up the paper cylinder, the projected spaces become much longer. This has ever been one of the cartographer's problems. It explains why you always take latitude/longitude and distance measurements at a point opposite your mark on the chart and also shows why vertical seamless cartography is very difficult, even with the mathematical and geometrical drawing wizardry of modern computer techniques.

If you add to these potential sources of error the fact that most hydrographic services only guarantee the accuracy of the passage charts (as opposed to harbour plans) to 0.1 nm, it is a miracle that any of us find our way around the oceans.

Even electronic navigation should sometimes be seen as an interpretive art rather than as a very precise science. When you recall that some GPS receivers give readings to three decimal places, you see how many of us delude ourselves into thinking that we are better than we are.

The Nautical Mile

If you wish to be pedantic, the nautical mile is the approximate distance in feet between two points on a meridian (that is, a north/south line on the chart), with their latitude separated by one minute of arc. Because the Earth is not completely spherical, this length varies from 6,046 feet at the Equator to

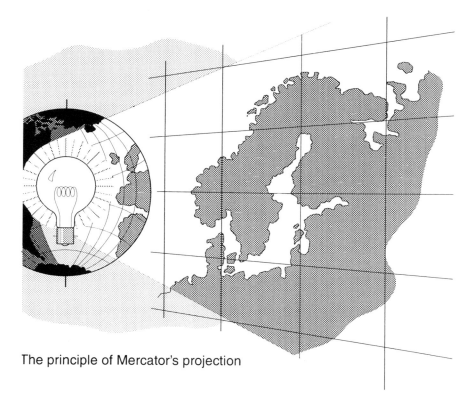

The principle of Mercator's projection

11.3 Even electronic navigators need to understand Mercator's projection.

6,108 feet at the North Pole. The mean is 6,077 feet, so for the sake of easier mental arithmetic most mariners calculate that 6,080 feet equals one nautical mile and the international nautical mile is 1,852 metres.

The third decimal place equals one thousandth part of a sea mile or 6.08 feet. On a passage chart, even the best navigator with new, sharp dividers would not be able to plot such a tiny distance and even a plotter cursor would cover a greater cross section. The larger scale charts in my portfolio (both electronic and paper) are to a scale of 1:12,500. Reduced, this means that 0.1 inches (1/10th) on the chart equates to 104 feet, or roughly 35 yards. Even that is quite difficult to plot.

Like the rest of us, the chart plotter designer and the electronic cartographer need to take these difficulties into account. Even though they do not add up to much, they do introduce an element of confusion – a fuzz factor – to navigation and can create the need for a lot of geometric tinkering when all your navigation is being done from GPS to paper chart.

As we briefly mentioned, the leading maritime and ocean survey nations have sensibly agreed to redefine all their charts to WGS84, but this will take a long time. The companies already engaged in converting paper to electronics have a distinct time advantage here. As they have built up their own libraries from scratch, they have mostly applied the datum corrections, but they also adopt the belt and braces insurance of quoting the derivation data on the chart itself.

C-Map NT technology, for example, has all charts drawn to WGS, but also has a menu saying which hydrographic authority produced the basic data and how long ago. This is displayed as an on-screen panel. It makes life much less confusing and is clarified even further because the new breed of plotter displays the charts in the actual 'cobalt and custard' colours used by the Admiralty whose charts are arguably the most respected in the entire world.

Still not Convinced?

I think that I shall very cheerfully strangle the next Luddite who tries to put me down by bragging that he still does everything with his sextant, then follows the boast with the question 'Don't you feel a great satisfaction when you have navigated, say, from the Solent to the Exe and you have done all the sextant calculations on paper and you are only 1 mile out – less than 1 per cent – when you reach the Fairway Buoy of your destination?' (Even if the cloud clears to let you get sight of sun or star and the sea is calm enough to let you align a horizon.)

The answer is 'No! I have done that' but now, to reiterate the fear, if there is a sea sensation worse than not knowing where you are and what is under the keel, I prefer not to experience it. On the other hand, I have plenty of sympathy for those who place their trust in paper charts and who are more at home with the panoramic view which their size allows. Just because you have added an electronic dimension to your navigational armoury and range of personal skills, this does not mean to say that you have to sell all your paper charts, or that you must forget how to use ruler and dividers.

All our own passage planning is done on the paper chart and then transferred to the electronics. If there is ever a discrepancy concerning, say, the course, or the distance between two waypoints, it is almost always that I have tapped a wrong key when inputting data.

The Halfway House

There is an in-between stage represented by such puck-driven plotters as the Vision and the long-established Yeoman. Both rely on referencing the puck's electronics on the printed grid lines of any chart. When the puck is moved, the position co-ordinates of its centre are displayed on its mini screen.

If the puck-plotter is interfaced (snob word for connected) to a GPS receiver, a traffic light system indicates when it is close to the GPS position, or precisely located over it. This method makes some navigators feel more secure because they have more control of what is happening and can actually see it evolving. Me? I enjoy navigating, so I like both systems and would have both if wheelhouse space and bank balance would permit.

We Live in Exciting Times

It is a personal opinion that those who do not take advantage of modern navigation systems are missing a lot of fun and denying themselves a great deal of sea safety. The antis generally cite fear of breakdown as the main reason for their mistrust. The counter argument is that you do not expect your digital watch to malfunction and you have complete faith in air travel, where all navigation – and even landing the aircraft – is now done entirely by electronics.

I derive great pleasure from owning a chart plotter. Not only does this pull me more often to the chart table, but it also extends my cruising season into the winter, when I can display charts both on the plotter and on the computer screen and can even type up my route of waypoints and pass them between these machines. Yet, I am far from being a computer/electronics expert, other than having the journeyman's skills which I have picked up on the boat and in the office. Winter navigation on dry land is huge fun. My next summer's passage from Brixham to Menorca is already being set into the machines. If I have to divert, it will be done very rapidly and very accurately, because the contingency plans have been calculated and typed into the electronic storage in the month of January, ready for an April departure. I might not use them, but I enjoyed creating them and will be safer and have greater peace of mind on passage, because they are already *in situ* and are available for very rapid recall.

11.4 Such a plotter is a valued crew member.

Final Persuasion

Had I not been an admirer of chart plotters and electronic cartography, I would have been instantly converted during last year's 150-mile passage from Southern Ireland to the Isles of Scilly. We embarked on this projected 30-hour trip south against the promise of a southerly, headwind of force 5 maximum for the last few hours. That would not be a real problem.

When we still had 70 miles to go the wind, unexpectedly early, backed south and increased to 45 knots. The boat coped remarkably well on a tiny portion of genoa, mizzen and engine. Conditions finally got so bad that the mizzen flogged itself to shreds, because it was then too dangerous to go out of the wheelhouse into the cockpit to take it down. We had to take the pressure off the boat (and especially off the crew) by turning the bows into the wind with the engine just nudging us ahead and the autopilot holding the course.

For some six hours, we steamed slowly away from our rhumb-line. It was even too rough to write up the log. The pencil would not stay in place on the paper. However, there was no panic, because the chart plotter showed our divergence angle and distance exactly. For safety, I periodically scribbled the time and the position from the plotter's digital display onto a pad, but this was about all I could manage. Plotting this on paper would have been impossible and it would even have been dangerous to stand at our chart table. On the one occasion I tried to do this, Neptune hurled me across the wheelhouse but – luckily – there was only minor damage to my pride and face, rather than, say, the catastrophic wrecking of an engine control, or pulling out an essential cable.

I did not enjoy this six-hour period, but when the wind moderated, I had an immediate on-screen picture of where we were in relation to our planned track and our destination. It took but a few seconds to draw a new electronic course line and to set the boat much more cheerfully along it.

Chapter 12

GPS – The Position So Far

The Navstar Global Positioning System (GPS) has been described as the next great public utility, destined to stand alongside electricity, piped water and the telephone as an essential and normal part of everybody's everyday life. Twenty years from now, that will probably be true, even though the satellites in use will not be military and will not be uniquely American.

The fact that GPS (or its future clones) has not reached a final development plateau and that the theory is moving much faster than the practice, explains the current GPS *status quo*, which is a confusion of politics, too much suitable and unsuitable equipment, with wild price swings compounded by sheer human greed, plus emerging, public body empire-building. Unfortunately for the end user, we who pay the piper cannot always call the tune.

To sort out the tangle, we really need to go back to that beginning when the US Department of Defense was only granted money for a sophisticated satellite navigation system, capable of giving extremely precise position fixes, anywhere in the world, at any moment of the day, on condition that the facility was also made available for civilian use.

This hyper-precision miracle was much too good to be solely the prerogative of the military. Remember that we who go to sea have long used the fact that every centimetre of the Earth's surface can be given its own unique address at a point where two fine lines cross, but only GPS has been capable of defining it with such accuracy and in terms of any time, any place and any weather, so the satellite system is ideal for our use.

Even the cheapest GPS receivers also display altitude, which brings the system into use for aircraft and for mountaineers. It is on land that most of the big money will eventually be made, but the necessary electronic maps are far from ready.

This unique address is not Mimosa Cottage, nor any other appellation understood only by locals, but an extremely fine-line grid intersection, at a very accurately measured distance north/south of the Equator and east/west of the Greenwich Meridian.

This is obviously latitude/longitude, or some sort of OS Grid, etc, but I still marvel that GPS can locate an antenna's tip to a spot defined even more precisely than three decimal places of a nautical mile (about 2 metres) using relatively cheap equipment able to demodulate signals from satellites circling 10,900 nautical miles above the surface of the Earth.

So, at sea, we have easier cartography and we are a safer sales target for GPS equipment not designed specifically for that environment. This adds to the confusion as the money moguls use the marine market as a sort of stepping stone to a land-based profit and are presenting us with a mixture of equipment which is excellent and rubbish. The US military have also gone only halfway by making GPS available but in a less precise and less consistent form.

Fortunately, there are many signs that things are beginning to change. There is much discussion about navigation aids into the next century and a great deal of political and commercial drawing-up of campaign lines. As always, it is left to the publishers – The Fourth Estate – to try to sort fact from fiction and to issue appropriate warnings. To do this, GPS – which is without any doubt where the future of navigation lies – must be seen *vis-à-vis* its rivals.

GPS versus the Rest

The Radio Direction Finding system (RDF) is now so little used that its imminent demise will not be regretted and RYA test candidates will no longer need to agonise over Morse Code – itself being phased out even by its military users.

The loss of Decca will be much more serious should its reliability, repetitive accuracy and familiarity be sacrificed on the altar of greed. Loran-C is the planned alternative and its selection will not surprise those who have followed the GLA-Racal Decca political in-fighting over the years. The last effort to foist Loran-C onto seafarers was largely defeated by the commercial fishing lobby, but the injuries still smart.

In technical terms, Loran-C is not as good as Decca. It operates in roughly the same frequency spectrum, so suffers similar weather and ionospheric shift problems. It

needs only one antenna to cover much of Northern Europe. This is currently sited in Southern Ireland, so will be at a greater distance from many UK receivers. In radio terms, increased distance always means lessened precision.

The only perceived advantage of Loran-C is that it costs considerably less than Decca to install and to maintain. It has absolutely nothing else going for it and somebody should point out that if we fear that the US is a foreign power and might unilaterally shut off GPS without asking the UK, we should remember that Southern Ireland is also a sovereign power with the same prerogatives.

Aficionados used to argue that Loran-C possessed the virtue of being the one system that could be used worldwide. However, much of the Mediterranean Loran-C has closed and even the US is shutting off Loran-C in the year 2000. Worse, it is now quite difficult to purchase Loran receivers in UK, so why are we bothering? Most of us will continue to ignore it because it has absolutely nothing in its favour.

So, satellites it is. Whether it be GPS, or paid Differential GPS, or the promised 'free' DGPS, or the vague plan for a Euro GPS system to be operational by 2000 – or should that read 2010 at the earliest? The argument that Europe needs its own satellite system to safeguard a USA switch-off, holds very little credibility. GPS is now owned 50/50 by the US Departments of Defense and Transport and so much civilian traffic is now dependent on it that a switch-off can only be ordered by Presidential Decree, probably because of a major war – when America would ask its allies to close their systems too.

The technical basis of GPS depends on super-accurate clocks and an engineer's almanac of where each satellite is at any moment of the day. Put very simply, the atomic clock out in space and the less costly, less accurate clock in the GPS receiver are made to generate the same signals at the same time. Bear in mind that we are talking about millions of radio-electric style pulsations every fraction of a second. The signals are called pseudo random codes, but there is nothing random about their pattern, nor in the way in which the receiver slides them around to find a match. When it does, it can 'look up' the time that the particular segment was transmitted and balance this against the time it was received in order to calculate how far it has travelled and – hence – the distance from satellite to ship. Radio signals travel at 163,000 nm per second and (at this ultra-high frequency) are not subject to much interference. Normally, a GPS antenna will be able to see six satellites and can choose the best three or more to get the navigator's classic cocked hat. Nothing incomprehensible so far.

Unfortunately, in the 0.06 seconds which it would typically take a signal segment to descend to Earth, the satellite would have moved about 200 metres. The calculation's reliability might also be degraded because the clock in the boat GPS is either a little fast or slow. These clocks are good, but are not infallible. If one is 0.001 seconds out, this would give a posfix inaccuracy of 163 miles.

About here, the wonders of high-speed data processing take over as the GPS receiver's computer looks at all the possible aberrations. It begins by rejecting co-ordinates which are plainly nonsense because they are, say, out in space. Then it goes to work on the very large cocked hat created by clock inaccuracy. By reducing the separate arcs by the same amount each time, it eventually locates the only possible spot where/when they can coincide. This is done

at a speed which the human mind is completely unable to grasp, but is very precise and once the computer has stored the amount the fix is out and in what directions, it applies this correction to all other received signals, until another major error is sensed.

Confusion Begins to Reign

So far, we have covered that part of GPS which is available to civilians. Beyond this Coarse Acquisition (CA) signal there is an ultra-sophisticated Precision level (the P code) of pseudo-random codes which are so complex that there is no danger of them being 'cracked' by any outsider. To get at this very fine tuned position-fixing system, the military GPS system needs to lock on by using the CA code, then switches to the P code when it has established an approximate position. This applies especially if the receiver has been moved whilst switched off.

The CA code accesses the penalty area, but

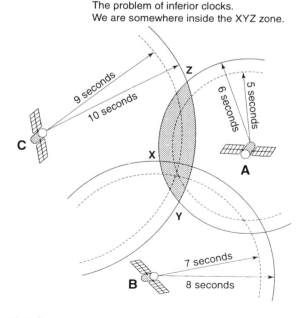

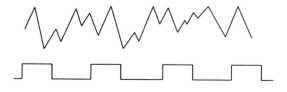

Representation of pseudo-random codes

12.1 Shifting pseudo-random codes.

12.2 Small time difference creates large position fixing error.

only the P code will find the penalty spot.

Unfortunately, the military under-esti-mated the design capabilities of civilian engineers, who began producing GPS sets so good that they were getting very close to the penalty spot, even using CA code messages. During the Gulf War, many Operation Desert Storm tanks were fitted out with Garmin, Trimble, Philips and Magellan equipment, because purely military gear was in very short supply. At that time, GPS was behaving so well that we were blown down through the notorious, fog-bound Chenal du Four knowing that our position was precise to 15 metres, but fearing for the accuracy of the charts and the confusion about which datum points they were drawn from.

Selective Availability

The jealous military were not happy about this freely available 15-metre precision. For reasons which centred on a fear of terrorists and of trigger-happy litigation, which might be initiated if somebody puts a tanker aground and tries to blame the navigation system, they decided to degrade CA accu-racy. In effect, they make the satellite clocks randomly tell very small fibs about the signal release time. In practice this lessens the accu-racy from a circle of 15 metres diameter to one of 100. The pleasure of Selective Availability (SA).

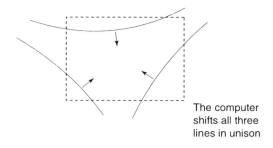

The computer shifts all three lines in unison

12.3 The computer reduces all arcs simultane-ously until a matching point is located.

Precise information about the current precision percentage is quite difficult to come by, apart from official and researcher mumblings that it is 2 drms. In practice this means that you always know that you are somewhere inside a circle 200 metres across. For a minimum of 65 per cent of the time the circle of imprecision decreases to 100 metres diameter – or 50 metres from your exact posi-tion.

These are the worst percentages. My own user-informed guesstimate is that GPS is more consistent than these figures, but that does not remove the need to treat satellite fixes with a touch of caution when you are close to hazards. Then it is better to believe the more cautious 'official' line that precision will be better than 100 metres for 95 per cent of the time.

At sea, you always know that you are somewhere inside this 200-metre circle, but can never be sure whether you are in the centre, or out towards the perimeter. For most of the time this does not affect naviga-tion which is backed up by traditional skills, but when the ostensible, GPS-derived posi-tion suddenly leaps from one side of the circle to the other, the computer deduces that the boat must have, say, slowed down, so indicates this at the display. It is SA which makes a total nonsense of GPS speed infor-mation. Even in the stillwater of a canal, or a lake, when we know that the boat is doing exactly 5 knots, the GPS speed read-out jumps about over the range 3.5–7.5 knots.

So What?

However, does the seafarer really need to be too bothered by this? In most cases, to know where I am to within 100 metres, in a fog, in the middle of the Bay of Biscay, at any time of any day, is still a comforting wonder. Closer to land, the old, tried and trusted tech-niques come back to the chart-table and the view from the wheelhouse window.

Differential GPS Precision

If we require greater precision than this, it is available – at the price to install Differential GPS (DGPS). Again simplistically, an interfaced GPS receiver and a sophisticated computer are sited at a location whose co-ordinates are known to a few centimetres. The raw GPS signals are processed to recognise the amount of, say, Northing and Easting error. This anomalous figure is corrected and the new, accurate figure is transmitted, by an independent radio link, to the boat GPS receiver, so that the correct position is displayed on the screen.

What you must pay in order to get this exactness also adds to the confusion, because there are a number of options. The broadest is the so-called 'free' or IALA system currently available in most of America and much of Scandinavia and Northern Europe. You pay extra for a decoder box and a beacon antenna, but there is no licence fee. This will give 2–15 metres accuracy depending on where you are.

Selective Availability's reduction of reliable GPS precision to within a circle of 200 metres diameter for 95 per cent of the time, but getting inside 100 metres for 65 per cent plus of the time, has been given enough airing. It is strongly rumoured that SA will be progressively phased out, which would make sense now that it is so easy to over-ride. This would restore 'raw' GPS to a positional accuracy of 15 metres from the true target spot, which is brilliant for 99 per cent of usages and even much too precise for most of us, for a number of cartographic reasons, which we have discussed in earlier chapters.

The only way to test your own system for local conditions is to remain in one location with a good GPS receiver and a chart plotter running continuously in tandem. My own observations lead me to believe that my home port chartlet is out of datum kilter by some 80 metres south. Even worse was a week anchored in Porto Colom (Balearics) when Pakman – our Chartnav's flashing position cursor – jumped ship and spent the whole seven days circling around a building site some 250 metres east of us. The chartlet was patently in the wrong place.

However, for general cruising, using GPS together with other navigational skills, I am still very happy to have it aboard and will be even happier if sense prevails over the SA nonsense. If a Euro system happens, that will also be fine, but I am not holding my breath.

Differential GPS is super-accurate. I was recently on a boat whose skipper put me over a table-sized rock in the tide rip of Poole Harbour entrance. We steamed a big circle and returned on the GPS numbers. When we took the towel off the video echo sounder, the rock was right beneath the boat again. The DGPS was confessing an accuracy of 3 metres and land surveyors get even closer.

Equipment Progress

The whole GPS concept has come a long way since 1991 when I paid £1,200 for my first Garmin Pronav – a tiny box with superb technology for its day and still working well now. At that time, buying GPS equipment was relatively straightforward. You either bought something like the Garmin, which had one receiver and some clever 'sequential' software, or you paid double this price for a multi-channel receiver. There was not much inbetween, which contrasts with today's plethora of suppliers, with its maze of receiving and interpretation systems and trade names, confused by a price range from £195 to £1,995 and beyond for what appears to be the same tool.

So What Do You Get For Your Money?

Firstly, if you believe the brochures, you will not nowadays get a single- or two-channel sequencing unit, because the manufacturers have changed the terminology, because they feared that it smacked of inferiority and to disguise the fact that they have devised some very clever software to improve the ability of the lower priced GPS to emulate multi-channel performance.

If you merely wish to know your position and do not mind it being displayed in small digits and are travelling slowly (at about yacht speed) there is not much user-discernible difference between the cheapest sets and the more expensive. Some lower- and middle-priced machines actually use the same 'engine' or 'chip' as the big boys, but as soon as you want more than the basic level of data and assistance, you begin to pay more.

Display Screens rule

One feature which certainly puts up the price is the size and clarity of the display screen and the sharpness of the digital and graphic shapes it shows. The Philips AP6/AP10, the Trimble NT200 and the Leica (which used to be Magnavox) are amongst the most expensive GPS units, but less costly rigs cannot equal their display screens.

The Disappointing Handheld

At the cheaper end, you are generally talking about handheld rigs with very small screens and a low pixel count, which show horizontal lines as zigzags and a slope as a staircase. Typically, such a display will measure some 40 x 60 mm (against 70 × 135 of the AP6) so cannot really compete. Even though these mini units boast such features as a 'plotter' with adjustable parameters, no serious navigator can pilot a boat on a screen measuring only 1.5 inches by 2.75 inches.

We are often asked if a handheld GPS will function down in the saloon of a yacht. The best answer comes from an honest salesman, who always replies by simultaneously saying 'yes' with his mouth and shaking his head to say 'no'. He means that it will work 'after a fashion', but to be certain, you need to hold it out in the open, where it has an unobstructed 360-degree view of the sky. Below deck performance varies from boat to boat, but will never equal the clear view antenna.

12.4 Our own big GPS screen would be difficult to better.

The only real solution to interior short-comings is to add an external antenna, but this can cost you say £50 to £130 even before you realise that many claims for battery life prove to be so fictitious that you scurry off to add a 12v supply cable and a fixing bracket – budget about £55 to £65 for them. These extras can mean that you actually pay a higher price for an inferior product, so it is not surprising that some suppliers are abandoning the handheld GPS market for the technical reasons above and because commercial viability depends on volume sales, which only appear to be achieved by the three dominant handheld companies. The news that some of these are to convert to twelve-channel technology will improve the unit performance, but will probably have a balancing effect of reducing battery life. Again, it should be stressed that most GPS money will be made on the land and this must remain the prime target for development and sales of handheld GPS manufacturers.

The Channel Problem

Having a six- (or even a twelve-) channel receiver means that you have six separate GPS, computerised radio receivers built into the machine. These handle the workload of acquiring new satellites, monitoring them, up-dating the almanac, reporting on unhealthy 'birds' and tracking routes, etc much more smoothly and certainly than a less powerful model.

A three-channel GPS will typically have two channels tracking satellites by 'sequencing' around them at fifty times per second, whilst the third does the 'house-keeping' of almanac and data processing. It does much more 'averaging' and 'estimating' to achieve its fixes. The obvious analogy is between having a boat with a three-cylinder diesel 'thumper' and being eased along by a smooth eight-cylinder super-charged job. The uninitiated will not notice much difference, especially when going slowly, but when speed significantly increases, or there is extra work to be done, the better quality shows.

The two occasions when inferior performance shows on the screen are: when a satellite drops below the horizon and the less costly GPS momentarily locks up whilst it searches for a replacement; and if you are using a GPS to drive a chart plotter. The cursor position of the multi-channel rig is much more stable than its inferiors. This also shows in the speed display. Expensive GPS units are fitted with a sophisticated Kalman filter which removes much of the signal-degrading radio noise and has a smoothing, or imperceptible averaging effect.

The Muddly Middle

The price and quality poles (£199–£1,999) are easy to perceive, but most of us get lost about value for money in the middle price range and are utterly confused by such trade names as the Garmin Multitrac 8 and Magellan's Allview 12. The question we are most frequently asked is 'If I cannot afford one of the deluxe GPS models, should I buy Garmin or Magellan?' Ignoring the author's disenchantment with handhelds at sea, the answer is to buy the one whose display, menu style and buttons appeal to you most. In value for money and in performance there is nothing to choose between them and it is also now worth considering some of the well-engineered clones such as Micrologic.

An expert airline captain cruising at 500 knots might spot some performance differences between Leica, Philips, Garmin and Magellan, but the yacht travelling at 6 knots will not notice much variation between them in the simple terms of pure speed of data processing and steadiness of signal.

As far as we are able to ascertain from the jumble of trade secrets, the Garmin, with its Multitrac 8 technology has a single 'receiver', which the company is anxious to differentiate from a 'channel'. It is supported by some exceptionally sophisticated software. It claims to do with software what others do with hardware, but in a totally different way. Like all GPS sets, it downloads the almanac of available satellites' bearing and elevation, then goes looking for the quartet with the best signal strength. Under normal conditions there are always eight possible satellites available, but some may be screened by hills, buildings, etc.

The Garmin software monitors three satellites for a horizontal fix and one for altitude and 'keeps an eye on' the others, ready to switch when one of the four in use drops out of view. The need for one channel to do all the work means that the displayed position is derived from more forecasting and averaging than is the case with a multi-channel machine. In theory this is not as slick, but in practice our yachtsman at speeds below 20 knots will not be able to discern any difference in the Garmin system. This certainly applies to the new twelve-channel models, which locate and relocate at a staggering speed. They are an improvement, but the older technology will still be around for quite some time yet.

The Magellan range boasts Allview 12 as its technological trade name because, under occasional and exceptional conditions, it is theoretically possible to 'see' twelve satellites from some favoured locations. There is nothing shady about this appellation whilst the Fourth Estate keeps you informed of its limitations. No matter what you call the device, there are normally only eight satellites in view and your middle range GPS will either select the strongest four, or those with the best geometry, but it will not be using any more for pure position fixing purposes.

At the time of writing, Magellan appear to use a twin-channel sequencing engine and their own software, which is as good as any of its fellows. It performs as well as any of the more common GPS receivers offered into the middle price range of the marine market.

The Status Quo

We who buy GPS for boat-use are currently enjoying and suffering an *embarras de richesse* which is following the same path as the computer trade. Some of the first equipment on the market remains in production and enjoys Rolls-Royce quality and reputation without now reaching RR prices. Then there is a second wave of good quality gear, very diverse in colour and appearance, but very similar in what it will do. Wave three is when the Far Eastern clone engineers finally catch up with technology and introduce products which are not always comparable in pure engineering terms, but are – nonetheless – fair value for what they cost and how long they will last.

Your Choice

So, it does not matter whether you buy on price, or because console space is limited, or if your main criteria for choice is quality and versatility. There is currently something for everybody. And the range of peripherals is ever more increasing. The watchwords will ever be the need to read the brochures carefully and to keep your wallet in your pocket until you have asked all the questions which this book should formulate in your enquiring mind.

Chapter 13

The Inevitable . . .

Right here is where the author comes out of that shell of anonymity in which he is a third party interpreter of systems and facts and must put all his cards on the table.

My hand reveals that I like computers and have that competence which comes from using them every day, but I still find them interesting. Even after a decade of daily work and play, I remain fascinated by the speed and the power which they bring to complicated tasks. For professional reasons, on our motor-sailer, we carry two notebook (laptop) computers with impressive specifications, plus a palmheld computer, which can connect to a mobile phone and fax and also perform many other boat-management functions. There is also a 128 Kb electronic organiser with several computing capabilities.

In marine terms, this armoury can perform, or assist with, many essential ship tasks: navigation; weather recording; general ship management; talk to GPS and plotter; store charts; display accurate charts; calculate tides for the next decade and 700 harbours; plan cruises; maintain databases of boat spares and serial numbers; and handle the cruise accounts, etc. It is also a lot of fun.

It is true that much of this work can also be performed by books and paper – if you have the room to store it all. It is also often quicker and easier to pick up a book, or a piece of paper if the computer is not already running, so we need to strike a balance between electronic wizardry and plain commonsense. Even an experienced computer mariner must remain aware of the limitations, plus the occasional data impermanence, or unreliability, which a combination of operator error and mis-keying imposes. Nor should we forget those breakdowns, which the sea occasionally forces on delicate electronics. He should be equally aware that much of his safety and success at sea are decided by the efficiency of the training and the planning ashore. This last is where the computer has much to offer.

For the moment, we must accept that, once they are at sea, there is a vast gulf between what the computer can do for big ships and what is possible on small leisure craft. There are also two very distinct and disparate sides to marine computer life, that is, what it can do out there on the water and what is possible on dry land. The shore and the sea. For the smaller yacht, shore-use currently has the edge, but things are certain to change.

If you are aboard a commercial vessel, or a

warship, the computer presents no problems. The environment is usually relatively stable and dry and the hardware can enjoy the increased security of mains voltage supply. Electronic data handling is now so sophisticated that some ships are not even bothering to carry a portfolio of paper charts. Their computers are 'marinised' but, because of the much softer working conditions mentioned above, they differ very little from office machines.

Boats shorter than, say, 45-foot, especially sailing boats, pose plenty of computer hardware problems, both in terms of vulnerability to seawater and damp air and there is also the constant fear that somebody will shake a wet hat, or an anorak over the keyboard. Only rarely have I seen a cruising yacht with enough space and such a real need to go hi-tech that fixing the computer in a permanent and solid place was the best navigational set-up. Not being able to have a permanent on-board installation, we have tried a dozen solutions with clamps and bungey cords, but none of them removes the apprehension when the boat begins to pitch and roll.

The person contemplating a computer for marine-use must do plenty of research beyond the sales spiels of hardware salesmen and the software vendors whose products are essential to make the hardware work. We were appalled to be told by a leading software supplier that our very expensive laptop computer would be perfectly safe held on the chart table by bungey cords or even Velcro. We pointed out that we had tried this, but do not do it any more because it does not work. In harbour there is no problem and in some sea states it survives. However, when the boat rears up and comes smashing down so that every rivet shakes, gold tip connectors come adrift and hard drives give up. Our contact asked how many times this had happened. Our reply, 'Once, about four years ago' was greeted with derision and the comment that 'Only once in four years. That is not too bad.'

It could have been catastrophic had we been out on a rough night, in some busy shipping lanes and lost the plotter, GPS, radar and even the engine instruments because a computer could not stand up to the conditions. We do not do it any more because once is once too often.

The anecdote is related to make the point that you cannot always trust 'so-called' experts in what is still a very developing field. There is no substitute for marrying your own experience and a large dose of commonsense, with extreme financial prudence and some third party knowledge from suppliers. Any other cocktail could be very expensive and leave a nasty taste in your mouth.

The other problems arise from the machine's preference for a smooth and stable power supply (that is, one with a very even sine wave output) which connotes extra cables. Also, the need for peripheral hardware (printer, modem, etc) equally creates difficulties, because they also require connector leads, cables, power supplies, etc cluttering up the boat and being a perpetual hazard for failure and ever in danger from passing feet.

There is always plenty of sailing club bar excitement when people begin to talk about the potential which a seagoing personal computer (PC) has for performing boat tasks, but this enthusiasm soon diminishes with experience. Those yacht skippers who hold club house court about the marvels of their on-board PCs, are rarely renowned for the number of times they go to sea, nor for the passages they undertake.

The Things to Come

At my last count, there were thirty-seven firms identifiable as working on marine software, but I could only find four who were trying to design sea-compatible computers (hardware). This is the most important next step to take and is beginning to happen, especially for larger leisure craft. It has been given a boost by the European appearance of several machines designed for the US military and having tough specifications to match the expected treatment on the battlefield.

The computer in Figure 13.1 is representative of one of the shapes of things to come. It has a tough, contrasting, very readable screen of sufficiently large dimensions to be practical and it is worked by a remote keyboard, which can be tucked away in its own drawer.

At the moment, there is still the problem of connection points for the input and output ports, so these are protected by a waterproof cover, but this is only effective when such peripherals as the printer, or the linkage to the radar and navigation system are not in use. There is also the deterrent of high cost, with many owners questioning whether they can justify an extra gadget which might retail at more than 10 per cent of the value of the boat.

The Computer at Sea

These things said, if you have the wherewithal to equip your boat with a purpose-built PC, you would be silly not to enjoy its powers. Electronic charts are just one example of the way forward, which even leisure boats will eventually take, not only for the reasons of their super clarity, but also for easy storage, rapid on-disk up-dating, safety and versatility.

Typical of the way technology can work, was demonstrated when a Scottish fishing

13.1 Aqualogic computers.

trawler broke down beyond emergency repair at sea, so had to be towed to the nearest port, where major surgery could be performed. This was a long way from the boat's home base and well away from its normal haunts, so the crews did not have the relevant charts on-board. They were essential, because the approach and entrance to the chosen port of refuge were both narrow and hazard strewn. Fortunately, the trawlers were well equipped and were able to receive the necessary charts direct from the Admiralty via the mobile telephone and some download-enabling software built into their computerised navigation system.

This incident illustrates the growing paradox of computers and the sea in that, even though they are conceptually complex, they can perform amazing things with apparent ease and with very simple operator skills. A favourite example of this complexity making life safer and simpler is the system allowing the super-imposition of the radar picture directly onto the PC screen.

The Horizon 3D is the embryo model of how many of us will navigate our cruising and fishing boats in the future. It is certain to be copied and the method will replace many of our current exciting individual, stand-alone systems – radar, instrument bank, chart plotter, GPS receiver, fish-finder – which have developed along their own separate lines, by pulling them all onto one display, or one computer screen display and its back-up.

The Horizon 3D radar and Chart System

In a nutshell, H-3D is a method of laying a radar picture over the more sophisticated electronic charts, themselves acting as a medium for a GPS-driven position plotter and track tracer, but with no aspirations to take the control of the boat away from the skipper. This retention of humanity arises because the design team was led by sailing people who are computer experts, rather than being computer nerds who can see

money draining out of the sea and who chase after it even though their boat experience is not great.

Once the principle of the boat computer is accepted, it makes sense to use its superior screen qualities for other displays and to have the radar picture on a PC screen is marvellous. It can be sited where it best suits the skipper and even be in a position remote from the keyboard, or mouse control. It can do away with the bulk (and cost) of a CRT radar display and makes multiple repeaters easy to install. My own preference would be to keep the trusted technology of the conventional radar display – but to let the computer do all the fancy stuff.

The Radar Interpreter

The H-3D radar interpretation is both powerful and simple to use (we are back to our paradox again). The very clear, colour screen of a normal monitor, or the superior TFT (thin film transistor) of a good notebook PC, is flanked by familiar computer-style menus. The column on the right controls the usual functions of VRM, EBL, range, range rings, ship's head marker and sensitivities. You can also change the pulse length to get a better quality image according to range and set the radar to look further ahead (off-set) or to be orientated 'North Up' to coincide with the chart – either paper, or electronic. Even for a die-hard like myself, this gives much better control of the radar than I can achieve with the many knobs and buttons. Much more of the juggling and balancing of range, gain and tune are done by the computer software which, I have to admit, does it more accurately.

The best part of this left-hand menu is a very potent ARPA system (Advanced Radar Plotting Aid). When the cursor is 'clicked' on a radar 'blip', it surrounds the target with a red square, gives it an ident number and subsequently displays its course, speed and CPA – Closest Point of Approach to your own vessel – together with the time this proximity will occur. If the square changes to a triangle, the target is on collision course with you, but the ARPA can also distinguish moving targets and the fixed ones that you will hit. This can be done on a normal radar screen, but the computer does it much better.

You can change all this into 3D mode showing the echoes in the 'virtual reality' of a computer arcade game, including each target's probable navigation light configuration. I find this to be interesting, but not much of a contribution to serious navigation and is occasionally confusing.

Even in pre-ARCS days, the acquisition of a chart plotter totally altered the way in which I pilot the boat, but now it is even more practical fun to use. Before the screams start, I should say that it has not reduced the navigational skills I use and has even added some new elements to them.

Before electronics, navigation was a somewhat imprecise art, but is now a very precise science needing tools to match. This includes GPS, which in its present form would not currently be precise enough (because of Selective Availability) to take full advantage of the H-3D quality. Hopefully, this is about to change and will bring some sort of electronic chart and radar combination of the H-3D style within the financial and environmental scope of most of us.

So far, we have described a super H-3D radar interpretation system, marvellous charts and a good position fixing method. Put them all together and you have a complete navigation and pilotage system available on any of the boat's PCs.

Horizon in Full Mode

When the radar picture is overlaid on the chart, you create a display which – even on a dark night – is akin to looking out of the wheelhouse window on a fine morning.

If there are two channel buoys showing on the radar (orientated North Up) their image will sit exactly on top of their relevant symbols on the screen. If there is no symbol

beneath, it must be a ship and it can be visually identified without the need to make the traditional calculations of 'ship's head on 345 and the blip is 27 degrees off the port bow, so subtract 27 from 345 and his magnetic bearing from me is about 320'. Interpreting the nature of a target is a simple matter of look and see. The shape of the coast, as drawn by the radar returns, should also align with the chart shape, so bays and headlands can be very quickly identified with total confidence about correctness. This makes the sea a much safer place to be, without reducing the number of skills the skipper needs to have at his fingertips.

Currently, the drawback to all this is the cost and the need to install the best (generally most expensive) equipment. Horizon 3-D will work much better with a commercial radar's 1 degree horizontal beam width, than with the 6 degrees of some of the cheapest yacht radars. My own set's 2.5 degrees would be just about acceptable. Efficacy is also affected by the rolling and pitching motion of the boat, that is, as the motion occurs, the radar scanner moves with it and the screened image shifts away from the two buoys quoted in the example above. This present problem will undoubtedly be resolved by the development of some sort of averaging and centralising software similar to the Bottom Lock function of a fishfinder, with its ability to iron out inconsistent motions.

Similarly, some of the more expensive twelve-channel GPS units, together with their sophisticated signal filtering enabling them to choose the best satellites for geometrical alignment rather than selecting by pure signal strength, will give a smaller 'cocked hat' than cheaper models, which merely lock onto the four strongest signals, so these make better use of this super-system's capabilities.

The Horizon 3-D has been profiled here because it is the first on the market and has already passed through our hands. It stood up to our tests very well and will undoubtedly be much copied and much reduced in price, when it has been refined and detuned enough for injection into the volume sales which smaller boats connote. All marine electronics has always followed this path.

Whilst the computer is just beginning to have some uses at sea, it is already performing some Herculean marine labours ashore. This is especially true of training.

The Computer as a Radar Tutor

An example of computer training suitable for both amateurs and professionals is the Rasim radar simulator trainer (PC Maritime). This puts a radar screen simulation onto the computer screen and lets it run in apparent real time. The student has all normal radar controls relating to changing range, converting to North Up, etc and also has control of the ship's speed and direction.

The training lessons are based on Dover Harbour. Students drive a ship in and out as they wish and at a speed of their own choice. As the ship is made to go faster, so the targets in relative motion also speed up. The screen can be left devoid of other vessels, or they can

be added as you wish. The simulation is very real and looks little different from the radar screen on my own boat. It is fascinating to watch the position of the harbour wall and of other ships change as your simulated vessel is made to alter course. The program is so sophisticated that you can actually take a boat into the harbour, turn it and move it into the berth going astern. As a training aid, Rasim is excellent. It is also a lot of fun.

The Computer as a Skipper Trainer

Merchant shipping certification authorities are presently shifting their emphasis from purely theoretical written tests, based on situations which are very different when you meet them out on the sea, in favour of more practical tuition and assessment of competence. Again, electronics will be much to the fore, not only because the vessels of the future will be more and more electronically operated, but also because realistic artificial training aids are now available and good.

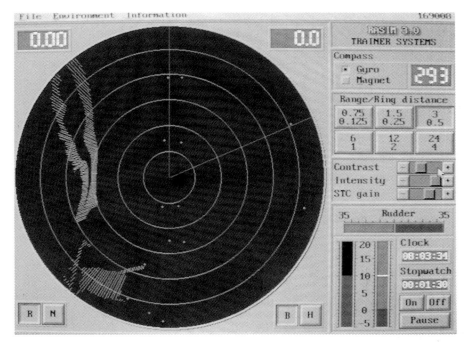

13.2 PC Maritime's Rasim radar trainer.

In this context, it is significant that over 50 per cent of an RAF fighter pilot's flight training is done on a simulator. If an airline pilot (even a very senior pilot) has not flown for a month, he is deemed to have lost his 'currency' and must spend time in a simulator cockpit to get it back. A personal friend, who flies very large long-haul passenger aircraft for a living, confesses that he is very impressed by how close the modern simulator is to the real thing. Sea training is already following this same path and what the professionals do today, then pleasure sailors – and the testing and licensing bodies who might control their destiny – will do tomorrow.

We saw this in practice during a visit to Plymouth for a viewing of the PC Maritime computer-based training program called Officer Of The Watch (OOW) whose pedigree is enhanced because it is already in use by the Royal Navy, RNLI, BP Shipping, US Coastguard, The Met and the training establishments of several other navies and shipping lines. It is a very impressive instruction medium, not completely virtual reality, but close enough to what happens in reality to give me several shots of real adrenaline when I thought that I was putting my simulated ship too close to another vessel, or onto a sandbank.

Officer Of The Watch and similar training programs, will not teach you to lay a boat alongside, nor to cope with wind and waves (only the sea itself can do that at the moment) but it teaches and tests just about everything else in a very real manner. Light recognition, collision avoidance, ship management, log keeping, radar techniques and good habits are all covered. If you think that PC-based simulations are akin to computer games, this one will make you eat your heart out.

At switch-on, the trainee and tutor decide what type of vessel they wish to be and are immediately presented with a typical set of bridge instruments and the sort of forward view you would get from the window. My first selection was to be skipper of a fishing trawler, whose panel on view was very different from that of the simulated container ship I tried later, which itself differed greatly from the yacht which I piloted to finish.

13.3 Officer Of The Watch trainer. You are a container ship skipper.

The training can then be as simple as what to do when meeting another vessel coming head-on in broad daylight, or as complex as having nine other boats steaming at different speeds and angles at night, with flashing buoys and shore lights tossed in to make the dish a bit more spicy. In normal operation, the other ships are programmed to behave correctly according to the collision regulations, but the tutor can also put in a rogue who seems not to have read the rule book.

Once the student is in control of his simulated ship, he can do a surprising number of very realistic things. Each of these actions changes the on-screen picture to resemble what happens in the real world. Turn the boat out to sea and you get a blank horizon. Come about and head for the shore and all the lights and other features come onto the screen and change relative to your forward, or side-looking window as it happens.

He can, for instance, look around a complete 360-degree field of view and have a very real picture of which vessels, hazards, weather and navigation marks are on either side, or even astern. He can turn his own ship and the view alters accordingly and is able to speed up, slow down, or go astern and the relative velocity of everything else changes accordingly.

If the naked eye is not good enough, the simulator skipper can pick up the binoculars and zoom in and out at will and has a hand-held sighting compass available. The radar is running and can be turned into a large part of the screen if the 'skipper' wants this. This latter is even more impressive than everything else and looks totally like the picture I get on my real world Raytheon and has all the same features and ranges, etc. Whilst all this is going on everything else is ticking away on screen: tachometer, speed log, echo sounder, compass, etc are all there.

There is a vast number of ways in which such a sophisticated training aid can be used to simulate what happens at sea. An experienced tutor can suggest corrective courses and speeds and the student will see their effect. This can be done in real time, or can be made to jump 5 to 10 to 15 minutes ahead and

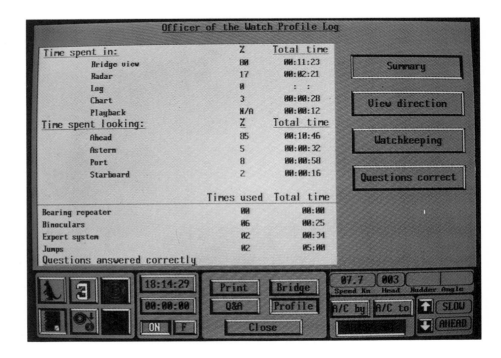

13.4 OOW keeps a computerised log.

the whereabouts of all the other screen features will change in lock-step. If the student is left to his own devices and rams somebody, that will also show in a definite manner.

To make life even more interesting, each and every student action is timed and recorded in an electronic log. At the end of the session, the tutor can point out that the simulator skipper ran into trouble because he only looked around once in 15 minutes, or did not consult the radar, or used the binoculars between 1015 and 1040, or that he speeded up to get across a slow-moving tanker, but forgot to take the revs off again. It happens.

This part of OOW could be used as an examination vehicle for many parts of tests leading to such qualifications as Yachtmaster, but it could not possibly replace certification (professional or amateur) decided by a test at sea. However, as a way of inculcating good habits in beginners, or – as in my own case – running a check to make sure that you have not become sloppy over basic good watch-keeping habits. But that is one of the strengths of the program. It is simultaneously a training aid, a test vehicle and a refresher course.

Another factor which I like is that being based on reality, you do not get a Clever-Dick, part-time examiner asking questions about abstruse situations and idiosyncratic light combinations, which crop up once a century and then smilingly patting himself on the back because you do not know the answer and he does – because he had the book to hand when he set the stupid question in the first place. The world of leisure certification is riddled with such theoretical anomalies. If and when universal training and examination comes, we must ensure that we are protected from this sort of egotism. It may well be that real-time, real-situation tuition and tests of the OOW-style will do that, especially if it is coupled with an assessment of the new watch-keeper's performance on a vessel, by a skipper known to be fair and honest about these things and who has no financial or personality axes to grind.

The Computer as a Planner and Ship Manager

So it is now possible to let the computer do a fair proportion of your crew training and bytes and chips can make a huge contribution to the actual handling of the boat. Because of its ability to crunch numbers, make rapid calculations and store vast amounts of configurable data in a small space, the computer is also an ideal ship management tool. It can be assistant navigator, bosun, purser, medic and communications department rolled into one.

However, before we get too hooked on computer power let us repeat and reinforce what practicality has to say. Suppose for a moment that I need just one fact like a passport number, a high water time, or the characteristics of a light. If I am at home, I need to leave my armchair to go to the room where the computer lives. On the boat, I must retrieve the computer from its safe and padded forepeak stowage, take it from its bag, plug in the power supply and be careful of the cable, switch on, wait for boot-up, locate the file and read it. Then I reverse the whole process.

In many cases, it would be simpler, easier and quicker to obtain the information from a book or a set of tables. I can do this right where I am and without fuss. If I shall require the data again, I need not copy it from the computer screen to the jotter pad, because the book will still be readily to hand.

The other side of the coin is the number of minutes – even hours – I have wasted turning the boat inside out to find a spare part, which I know to be somewhere on-board, but I cannot remember exactly where, so I turn out lockers, then repack them hurriedly and badly to make enough space to turn out the next and so on. At such times a good list could be a life saver. The trouble with lists is that you sometimes end up with bits of paper in a muddled pile. Every time the boat's manifest changes, or I find a safer waypoint, the pages become filled with crossings out, writings over and confusion. So you have to rewrite the whole page, which makes the book a mess.

This makes the computer very useful. Storing your original list is not a problem. When you write a new one, or change a route, you do not risk losing your old data through error, but make the alterations and store this revised version under a new name, or give it a higher numeric file suffix, for example, Stores.1, Stores.2, etc. The newer edition would also show by having the more recent date automatically recorded by the machine's operating symbol.

If you still feel that a laptop computer is still too troublesome and vulnerable to be a frequently used tool, I would go a long way with your argument. The alternative compromise between computer and inconvenience might well be one of the rapidly developing palmheld machines. We are not talking here about an electronic organiser, but about a tool which comes between it and a computer. A number of companies are developing very powerful miniature machines and these are finding increasingly useful places on boats which is, in turn, persuading people to develop software and other features specifically for marine use.

Psion were the pioneers of this mode and are arguably the world leaders. I have no particular brief for the company other than being the user of a Psion 3c, whose power and versatility constantly surprises me. It has a dedicated database for names, telephone numbers, etc and a diary section in which I note tide times for important days, etc. There is a standard calculator with a maths co-processor side and a surprisingly powerful word processor which will drive a printer. At 2 Mb, the storage is ample and it even has games of Patience and Scrabble to relieve the boredom of night watches.

Because this machine has no moving parts (all data is on solid-state, flash disks) the boat's motion does it no damage. It can be further protected by a leather case and can be used inside this cover, or mounted very safely on a dedicated clipboard, which has a convenient A4 pad beneath. The ensemble is easy to get out/put away so you use it more often. Mine has a power lead, but I have not used it since logging thirty-one hours actual running time on two ordinary A4 batteries.

Occasionally, somebody will complain about the small LCD screen and the tiny keyboard, but you can connect the palmheld to a standard PC to in-put and edit data on the larger keyboard and screen. With a PCMICA card and a suitable mobile phone you can also send and receive fax messages, or keep in touch with friends and clients via an e-mail address. This has the advantage of being usable at off-peak times to reduce expensive call-time when overseas.

And There's More

The on-board (mini) computer also has a number of boat specific uses.

13.5 The boat's Psion 3c showing waypoint list.

Expense Management

Expense management is an obvious function and there are many programs for all computers. I, personally, like to know how much a year I spend on fuel, repairs, berths, replacements, etc. There are some who argue that this knowledge could well frighten you away from boating. An acquaintance has calculated that every time he travels from his mooring to the Fairway Buoy, it costs him £4 per two-mile trip. If he went out more often, this average would reduce and would soon show up on the computer.

The Bosun's Locker

The bosun's locker program is just a word processor text file which lists the contents of every box and locker on the boat. It is a simple text file. When I need a replacement glow plug for the diesel engine, a piece of flexi pipe, or a rudder bolt, the program's search function soon finds it. You could also list all your spares with a key letter, or a symbol to indicate the storage space (1 = port-side cockpit locker, 5 = red-topped box, etc) and let the computer sort your list into alphabetical order. This could be printed and clipped into your boat data book.

The Larder List

The larder list is also a word processor file in tabular form. Because we are away for an extended period each year, we begin to stock up our larder from January onwards. Every time we go shopping, we buy a few non-perishable things for the boat's six-month summer larder. In this way, we avoid a huge pre-departure bill, especially for such expensive items as jars of coffee. The spread-over eases our finances and it is fun to watch the pile growing and seeing the items get filled in at their appropriate screen slots. The computer list can be compared and refined from year to year.

Equipment

Equipment is a database easily adapted from the one included with the Psion (Hewlett-Packard, Sharp, etc) and lists serial numbers, dates of purchase, costs etc for all electronics, cameras and the like. There is also room for passport, insurance and licence and registration details. The small machines makes these fast to access when we are visited by Customs officials, or when you are cramped up in a telephone kiosk.

The Pre-Launch Database

The pre-launch database should avoid the embarrassment of one year when we arrived at Audierne, only to find that a most important box of torches, flags, bicycle parts, etc was still sitting in the garage.

The present format is a small data card for selected activities. Thus, the one labelled Dinghy allows us to check off everything as we take the annual load out of a very untidy garage and move it to the yacht. There are also cards for Deck, Engine, Instruments, Rigging, Outboard Motor and so on. They are stored on the computer, but we also print-out a hard copy.

The Chart Library

The chart library and a computer database might have been made for each other. Ours is another ordinary word processor file, but it could have been adapted from an in-built version. It copes well with the sixty-plus charts which we already have. They are recorded according to age, latest correction date, serial number, name, scale and description, plus whether they are Admiralty, Imray and so on. If we lend charts to other people this is also noted.

Further, when time permits, a breakdown of the contents of our collection of chart plotter cartridges will be added. The C-Map electronic chart of east Spain and the Balearics, for example, contains ninety charts and chartlets – which is marvellous for a single cartridge, but the details are impossible to remember. They are listed in the catalogue, but this is too bulky to take to sea. If we wish to know whether a particular harbour is covered in detail, it will be a simple matter to reference the database.

Navigation

Navigation requires some extra software and the Glasgow company Maritek are the brand leaders for Psion hardware and marine software. We are currently running two very useful programs.

Navigator

Navigator is a very convenient way of storing all your waypoints (or fishing and diving marks) which can be edited at will and also grouped-up in routes. This is a good planning aid, thanks to a number of menus which give instant access to course and distance between any two waypoints.

You can also set in the boat's usual speed for any given wind strength and angle and make allowance for leeway and tides to plan a route and to calculate your ETA for any point along it.

An actual example that I am currently planning (in January) is a trip from Brixham to Bordeaux in April. The waypoints have been taken from the charts, or from the chart plotter and I shall not need to work them out again – especially if it gets rough and the chart and dividers will not stay still.

We need to arrive at Porsal, at the head of Brittany's Chenal du Four round about high water Brest, to carry one tide down to the famous Raz de Sein, to be taken at slack water low. The Maritek has calculated the time I need to leave Brixham (our average speed is 5.25 knots) to arrive on schedule. I like to have waypoints every 20 miles down the rhumb-line, so the machine also tells me when I should be at each of them.

I can do this on paper, but once I have assembled my data, there is no further need to strew the lounge floor with charts, but I will check our chart navigation against its electronic cousin when we are in the last throes of planning and setting up the plotter, etc immediately prior to departure. In January, I flip open the Psion and plan there and then. By in-putting all the diversion and refuge points, together with the latitude/longitude of hazards along the way, or marks which might be useful for compass bearings, I have a powerful armoury of information for position fixing, in addition to the peace

13.6 Maritek tide table.

13.7 Maritek tidal graph including a line indicating boat draught in relation to available water.

of mind of always being able to calculate the location of a hazard in relation to the boat.

Maritek can be interfaced to any handheld or fixed GPS and chart plotter and can pass to it all this data which has mostly been typed up on the office PC. I take a printed copy as back-up. *En route*, the program can act as a GPS display and will log changes of course and speed for retrieval to the log-book when things calm down.

Tide

Tide is one of my favourite Maritek programs (I also have it for a standard PC). It resides on a Psion solid state disk and will give the tidal data for any one of 700 harbours for any hour, or part of the hour, for every day of every week until AD2015. The information can be seen per day, or it can be printed as a monthly table, or shown as a graph/curve for the day. Smaller, in-between, harbours can be added but there are already plenty set up. The program gives three locations even for the River Exe.

As a planning aid, both long-term and as you approach a harbour this type of program is invaluable and when combined with the other features creates a very powerful, small to carry and easy to use boat management tool. Its popularity is certain to increase.

Chapter 14

Integration and All That

Integration and interfacing are two words which are an unavoidable part of the electronic seafaring vocabulary. In many senses they mean the same.

An integrated instrument is one which fits into a bank, or chain of displays. The normal arsenal of instruments to show wind speed and direction, water depth, boat speed and mileage covered, plus perhaps water temperature and rudder angle is usually where integration begins. The separate displays can be bought from a variety of sources, but it makes more sense to buy an integrated package. The units often share a common power supply and their data can be passed to a repeater, or have the main information elements shown at one multi-function display head.

Interfaced, in its simplest form, merely means connected to: you can interface almost anything with anything else on a high-tech boat. In theory you could interface the GPS with the autopilot and send it along a route of waypoints with nobody at the helm. It would even be possible to interface the radar with this combination, with a radar guard set so that the boat would put in a 'dodge', that is, make a sharp turn away from its course if a target comes inside the guard zone distance.

There are obvious problems to the totally un-manned ship, but to have only one man on the bridge of a cargo ship is now quite normal. To cope he relies heavily on electronic system interfacing.

Who Needs to Talk to What?

The commonest need for inter-system connection is best illustrated in Chapter 9, which discusses how all relevant data can be fed into one box and then passed out to whichever system needs it. Another example is to interface the radar with the GPS navigator, so that it displays the current heading, distance and waypoint information.

Some power boat owners interface the GPS and the autopilot so that the boat's heading is constantly being monitored and tweaked to point straight at the next destination. There are a number of apparent dangers in this, besides the fact that it diminishes that awareness which comes from surveying and driving the boat.

For a sailboat, or even a heavy displacement motor vessel, it can be an inefficient way to navigate. In wind and tide, you often get there quicker by allowing the boat to be pushed sideways by the tide, rather than constantly pinching up into it, which is what the navigator interfaced autopilot does.

Many of us who are electronics devotees acknowledge its clever power, but have no wish to abandon control to its blind, senseless pilotage. So we settle for putting all the data on the autopilot screen, or the repeater screen, but not in a manner to let one influence the functions of the other.

Instrumentation apart, the most common interfacing seen on leisure boats is between GPS and chart plotter. If the electronic cartographic unit was not fed data about the boat's position, you could still use it just as a chart, showing latitude and longitude and calculating the bearing and distance between points. However, unless the two are properly connected, you cannot see the boat's position on the screen chart.

The Disappointed

Properly connected is the key phrase in the preceding paragraph, because interfacing will only be successful if the two pieces of apparatus speak the same language. It may sound strange that inanimate devices should need a language, but this problem will be readily appreciated by computer users, few of whom will not have experienced the irritation of acquiring an exciting new program, but finding that the computer cannot read the language in which it was written.

Unfortunately, at the time when marine electronics was just beginning to experience the excitement of a surge of new ideas, with plenty of clever software, nobody thought to say 'Steady on chaps. It would be best if we all wrote our programs in the same language.'

A frequent *cri de coeur* on our own telephone is the unfortunate guy who has bought an expensive GPS from Company A and an equally expensive chart plotter, or radar from Company B, only to find that they cannot talk to each other.

This situation mostly happened by chance, but it also has to be admitted that some manufacturers deliberately write all their software programs in their own in-house language in order to tie a user solely to their products. The only solution is to recognise that you are imprisoned and hope for the best.

The alternative, for those who feel that they might like to be free to buy what they consider to be the best equipment, is only to buy units which speak the common international language.

NMEA 0183

The current universally-accepted communication method for electronic devices manufactured by separate companies and even assembled in different countries of the world is to use a data transference language devised and promoted by the (United States) National Maritime Electronics Association. We are currently on a version entitled NMEA 0183, which is normally spoken as its initials NMEA, or even called NEEMA183. It describes itself as an 8-bit ASCII, parity disabled, block orientated protocol for data transfer.

The definition is clumsy enough to be very exact and will not change much when we get onto NMEA 2000. ASCII is a computer language using binary codes standardised by the American Standard Code for Information Interchange. A protocol in computer language means a set order in which information is passed so that the recipient device knows to what the figures relate.

In many ways, that neatly encapsulates the understanding of NMEA 0183. It is a series of phrases transmitted from a Talker, to any number Listeners, in an agreed order, to make up a sentence. In dealing with the sort of information which an electronically-equipped boat might need to have passed to several instruments, it is useless to send the figure 10 if the computers do not know whether this refers to boat speed, wind velocity, or compass deviation.

NMEA 0183 equipment can decipher each message with no fear of ambiguity, because each segment of information is contained in a phrase and each phrase is not only given a numbered location in a sentence, but the phrases are also always transmitted in the same order. Each also has a unique identification symbol as the first transmitted byte. The phrases are separated from each other by commas and these are included in the message even if there is no data between them. So, by counting the commas and decoding each phrase's initial ident, a receiving Listener knows whether the incoming information refers to boat speed, or to wind, or to a waypoint destination. In addition to its own identifier, each sentence has a terminator – a back-up to everything else telling the Listener that a new information segment is about to begin. By this method, not only is data passed in general terms, but it can also have a specific address – for example, sending a change of compass course to an auto pilot, or giving a chart plotter information about a new route.

Once you begin to understand Neema One Eight Three, you begin to see what an incredibly unambiguous, versatile language it is and how much keyboard work and time can be saved by using it. The present software version can translate thirty-five different sentences, each transferring information about a different subject, varying from barometric pressure at sea-level, via true or apparent wind force and direction, up to satellite status, then even to let you know the time at which you will reach the next waypoint – with much more besides.

It also has a contribution to make to safety by decreasing the chance of an accident caused by navigational error. In traditional navigation, most errors are due to mistakes in arithmetic. Many of us, for instance, are not adept at working to unusual arithmetic bases, so we find it difficult to add and subtract hours, minutes and seconds, or to multiply in degrees and minutes, so we make mistakes. Many NMEA 0183 devices have an in-built calculator to do this for you and also to handle the very large numbers which confuse all but the mathematically-gifted.

In electronic navigation, other accidents happen because a careless operator activates a wrong key, or transposes two figures whilst entering data. Good units will squeal a warning and will even reject the input if it is very incorrect (for example, attempting to put a letter into a numeric field) but, in any event, as long as the operator has checked the information when it is put into the system, it will always be correctly passed from, say, GPS to autopilot, or to a repeater, no matter how many times it is used. Marine electronics obey the computer user's cliché that garbage in equals garbage out and the consequences can be very serious. The good electronic skipper is generally a very careful navigational planner, because he knows that correct usage makes him very safe and incorrect usage is dangerously the opposite.

This philosophy was recently borne out when we decided to leave St Peter Port at 0500 on a dark September morning and head north up the Little Russel into a rising wind. An operator who shall be nameless, but not blameless, entered the correct data into the GPS, but put the chart plotter cursor on the wrong channel marker. Unfortunately, we also did not obey our normal night passage rule that one of us always checks the other's plan and figures.

As soon as we got into the main channel, it was obvious that something was wrong. The lights and marks were not in the right relationship to each other. As long as we followed traditional, good seamanship practices, we were not in any danger and the hazards were showing clearly on the radar. We were just lost for a while and life was made more complicated because we could not immediately identify which of our information systems was at fault – plotter, GPS, eyes, or paper plot.

Eventually, by slowing down and going over the passage plan again, we spotted the error and a very embarrassed skipper (who shall still remain nameless) got us underway again after a delay of only five minutes. Once we had established our position and line to take, the sum total of the electronics kept us on line, even though it was pitch dark and beginning to get a bit choppy where the wind was over the tide. It is a good feeling when all the systems come together and are confirming each other's advice. We were safer with the electronics talking to each other than we would have been without them and, I confess, that because I do not know this interesting channel very well, I would not have taken it on in the total dark without my electronic crew members.

That night was one more proof that electronic navigation and having instruments which can tell each other clever things, does not remove the need for traditional seamanship skills. A poor navigator will be an indifferent pilot no matter how much electronic equipment you give him. Indeed much modern equipment (as illustrated in the incident above) not only sharpens the navigator's abilities, but also makes him learn new ones. Some understanding of how NMEA 0183 works is undoubtedly one of these.

Reading NMEA

The Neema sentence passing a position in latitude and longitude is a good example of phrases making up a sentence and can be seen from the block explanatory paragraph and the ensuing extra explanation.

$ The dollar sign is often used in computer language to denote the commencement of a new activity.

GP (GPS) is one of many abbreviations which are used in 'GPS speak'. They range from the esoteric WCV for Waypoint Closure Velocity to the commonly understood COG, or Course Over Ground, which will be familiar to anyone who has used Decca or other position-fixing electronics.

GLL is a sentence formatter which confirms which language is being spoken

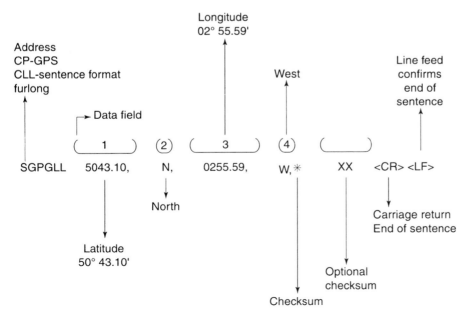

14.1 Typical NMEA sentence.

and which spacing conventions and symbols are to be employed.

A **data field** is a space between commas and carries actual navigational information, as opposed to other segments of the sentence which are giving instructions about how the sentence should be decoded.

Latitude and longitude are normally passed in decimal notation of degrees, minutes and decimal fractions of a minute (base 100 or 1,000) rather than degrees, minutes and seconds (base 60). It should be noted that many GPS receivers can calculate co-ordinates to three decimal places, or one thousandth of a nautical mile. This is of little value to the sea navigator, but has many applications in surveying. The on-board computers of a good GPS unit will rapidly convert base 60 readings to base 100, or vice versa.

Checksum is a computer tool often used to verify that a computer disk's information is correct and is here put in to ensure that the data is as it should be, that is, that a letter has not crept into a latitude field, which should only contain figures. It is always the last passive action agent of a Neema sentence and

is usually followed by the active instructions.

<CR> <LF> carriage return and line feed which are familiar to computer users in their overlapping functions of starting a new line and telling the printer to move the paper (or screen) up the measured distance to accommodate it.

The sentence described above is relatively simple in having only four data fields. The sentences giving the bearing to a selected Waypoint has twelve phrases in addition to its instructions and can even differentiate between those required for a Rhumb-line course, or for Great Circle navigation.

Conclusion

The electronic communication language you are using never comes to the surface unless you are a software engineer – and even the best of them are reluctant to tinker with it. Just as you do not need to understand all the workings of your car in order to drive it, so with marine electronics. But, just as you would not refuel a diesel car with petroleum spirit, so you need to be sure that all the driving and communications parts of your

14.2 NMEA sentences being passed from GPS to mini computer screen.

boat system are compatible with each other.

If you are unsure about reading the specification to check that your next purchase is compatible with what you already have, the safest way is to contact a member of the British Marine Electronics Association (BMEA, c/o British Marine Industries Federation, Meadlake Place, Thorpe Lea Road, Egham, Surrey, TW20 8HE. Tel: 01784 473377) whose members are all knowledgeable and all work to the Association's agreed Code of Practice.

It cannot be too strongly repeated that some 90 per cent of the queries of disappointment which cross our desk, come from boat owners who are having problems relating to instrument and instrument communications compatibility. Sometimes they are trying to get a system to perform a trick which is not in its repertoire. More often they are trying to force a marriage between incompatible partners.

The best way out of this dilemma is never to get in it. That simply means doing the research with known specialists before you sign your cheque.

Chapter 15

The Electronics Engine

Wise skippers reckon that a modern boat has two engines. It has a main motor which drives the boat through the water and a subsidiary bank of batteries which drive everything else. Volts and amps are now as much a part of normal seagoing vocabulary as bow and stern have ever been, yet many boat owners have a very insouciant attitude to their source of electrical power. As long as the thing is working, there is a reluctance to think about it until it dies and the engine will not start. Only the prudent seem to care about battery health and to run a check on this from time to time. They know that if a battery is feeling a bit unwell, all other dependent devices will also operate below par. For safety's sake, we should all become prudent.

A major cause of boat gear failure is very often not the equipment itself, but failure or other shortcomings in the amount and quality of the voltage being used to drive it. There are a number of reasons for inadequacy and a number of possible solutions.

Solution One: Better Batteries

The first need of an electronically well-equipped boat is good batteries. It is galling to look beneath the hatches of some very expensive yachts and note that the batteries are just a couple of over-the-counter jobs from the local hypermarket. We need to do better than that. To run our stable (listed in the Introduction) we are on three good quality batteries culled from the road haulage trade, totalling over 600 Ah. We could get away with less, but we have a source of good battery bargains and like to keep our refrigerator running non-stop, even in Mediterranean climates where the ambient high temperature makes it work hard, so we have installed the maximum. The Colvic Watson is a very tolerant load carrier, so we get away with it.

The lay-out is pretty standard, with one battery reserved entirely for engine starting and the other bank to serve the domestics and the navigation gear. However, during our season as live-aboards, we do not isolate one battery from the rest. We start the engine every day as a matter of test routine, so we leave all three batteries ganged-up, so that they all get their fair share of use. We have various recharging methods but, largely because of the refrigerator, need to run the engine for a while to restore this massive capacity.

Running a diesel engine unloaded is not really recommended by the purists, but more pragmatic engineers shrug and opine that it seems to do no harm as long as the revs are kept low and the alternator is providing some sort of load. They point out that many static engines run on low power, uninterrupted for decades.

Thanks to influences beyond the marine trade, the yacht skipper now has a number of interesting battery options.

The totally sealed battery offers the possibility of installation in unusual places without the danger of spillage and even though it has its critics, we have never had any problems with it. The new range of large storage nicads is pointing the way ahead, but it is currently (no pun intended) a bit too expensive for most of us. The more plebeian solution is for standard products with a good reputation, allied with careful monitoring and better charging.

The haulage trade is mentioned, because that is now the source of our batteries. Like all boat owners, we were originally seduced by the arguments in favour of deep cycle batteries. The protagonists (and sellers) correctly argue that standard car batteries are designed to take a very high load during starting from cold and are then rapidly recharged by the car's alternator. Because they are not intended for slow discharge over long periods, they react to this and soon begin to fail.

This argument ignores the changes which have taken place in road haulage. Truck drivers now expect to have a sleeper cab capable of running 12/24v lights, television, refrigerator and kettle. Engineers have designed land batteries to cope with this and to keep the cooler of a refrigerated truck running overnight without the need to run the vehicle's engine.

To achieve this, road haulage batteries have moved much closer to the characteristics of deep cycle cousins. So, if we were seduced by the warnings and the publicity surrounding special yacht batteries, we were soon jilted by a comparison of prices. Typically, we were asked for £240 (trade) for a 200 Ah deep cycle yacht battery, but obtained a 225 Ah truck battery for £80 inclusive. Two of these, together with a smaller version, have now been on the boat for three years without signs of problems. They are amazingly tough and appear to have withstood the abuse of a long season where the charging voltage had slipped up to 14.6 volts.

One reason that they withstood this trauma is that they are very large and are only large because I could afford them at the road haulage prices. Put another way, these costs either give me more power for less money, or I can ignore that they might not last quite as long as so-called deep cycle batteries, but can afford to change mine three times for the same outlay.

Proper Choice and Installation

I am grateful to The British Marine Electronics Association for permission to reproduce the advice from their handbook *Batteries – A User's Guide to Installation* (BMEA Code of Practice – second edition).

This article applies to lead acid batteries of the vented or valve-regulated type. Vented batteries are those that permit the gases evolved during charging to be vented to the atmosphere through the top of the battery. Valve-regulated batteries (sometimes called sealed batteries) have a valve on the top of the battery to reduce the gas evolution by about 95 per cent. The hydrogen and oxygen produced are recombined within the battery. Valve-regulated batteries cannot be topped up as the electrolyte reduces.

1.13.1

a) To calculate the battery capacity required it is necessary to establish the likely current demand and the duration that will be required when the alternator is not in use. If the boat is to have only one battery set, then the capacity calculation must include sufficient power to start the engine.

The formula to arrive at the demand is:

$$I = C/1.2t$$

I = Discharge current (Amps)
t = Time required by the user (hours)
C = Battery capacity stated by the manufacturer (Ah)

Generally, when being charged, batteries need 1.2 times their capacity to return them to their fully charged state.

b) Each battery should be provided with a durable label bearing the manufacturer's name, type number and battery capacity.
c) Batteries should be fitted so that they can be easily removed and the top of ventilated batteries should be easily accessible for checking the electrolyte level.
d) Batteries should be installed so as to restrict their movement horizontally and vertically. A battery should not move more than 10 mm in any direction when exposed to a force corresponding to twice the battery weight.
e) Batteries should be fitted in boxes or trays of non-corrosive material so that leakage of all the electrolyte from every battery in the box should be contained within the box to a level not exceeding 75 per cent of the height of the box.
f) Batteries should be capable of an inclination of 45 degrees without electrolyte spillage.
g) All fittings should be corrosive resistant and treated with protective material such as petroleum jelly or silicone grease.

1.13.2

a) Batteries should be located where they are not exposed to excessive heat, cold, spray or physical damage.
b) Batteries should be installed or protected so that metallic objects cannot come into unintentional contact with the battery terminals.
c) Batteries should not be installed directly above or below fuel tanks or fuel filters, or in the bilges.

1.13.3

a) Any metallic component less than 300 mm directly above a battery shall be protected with insulating material.
b) Battery cable terminals should not depend on spring tension for attachment to the battery terminals but should be of the pillar bolt or double screw type. Aluminium road vehicle type terminals are not recommended.

Solution Two: Better Monitoring

If better batteries are Solution One, the next step must be better current utilisation. Basically this means good wiring and contacts, keeping out corrosion and generally a bit of care to see that you do not get voltage loss in transit from battery to equipment and switching off the non-essentials.

Once a year, it pays to have a look at all the main connections, then remove any rust and *verdigris*, not only from the current-carrying lines, but also from any earthing straps, or from lines leading to sacrificial anodes.

One of our own best buys was a circuit and consumption monitor. In addition to showing battery voltage, it can also display the amount of current being drawn by any of the circuits which we have passing through four circuit breakers, This provides information which is both useful and essential. When we were going through the throes of ordering a solar panel, we required this knowledge to calculate how much power we needed to cope with the fridge, which comes on for five minutes, three times an hour and draws 5 amps. The monitor shows that if we put up all our steaming lights, they pull 11 amps and the autopilot demands 5 amps when it is on drive, but this is periodic and of very short duration.

It is also very prudent to carry an electrical test meter – ohmmeter or similar. There are plenty of cheap and very effective digital test meters available. They can perform some of the functions of the dedicated circuit monitor above in addition to being an essential diagnostic tool.

Our engine is old enough to need pre-heat from gloplugs. If the beast is reluctant to start, it takes but a couple of minutes to run the meter across the ends to ascertain if a shorted-out plug is the cause, or whether we need to look a bit deeper. Whenever we have an electrical fault, or are installing new equipment, the little meter is a constant companion and is especially useful when we wish to identify particular wires and circuits by using its continuity sight and sound signal. We also use plenty of nicad batteries for various torches, shavers and other gadgets whose health is greatly assisted by knowing when they need recharging.

This is accomplished via a 12/230 voltage inverter – a fit it and forget it implement. We opted for 200 watts, primarily to run our work computers and printer, but it also powers a number of kitchen implements, etc. With hindsight, I should have doubled the wattage.

If you are using the meter as a battery diagnostic, there is a good rule of thumb to indicate approximate battery state according to voltage shown:

12.2v = 50 per cent state of charge
12.4v = 70 per cent state of charge
12.7v = 95 per cent state of charge.

Solution Three: Better Charging

On our own boat, which is powered by a 50 hp diesel, when we isolate the single engine starting battery it is not a problem. It is hammered for a short period to get the diesel going and immediately revived by a hefty input from the alternator. Put very simply, it is not allowed sufficient time to develop any bad habits.

On many boats, the domestic pair can be bad news because they are subjected to regular long cycles of deep discharge at slow pace over a protracted period. This lets them fall into the very bad battery practice of dropping below 50 per cent capacity. The two side effects are the build-up of lead sulphate on the plates (sulphation) and an inherent resistance to re-charge (counter voltage). The problem is aggravated because a normal automotive alternator and regulator charges at a fixed voltage, so cannot really sense whether the battery needs more current or less current to achieve its optimum charged state. As a result, most boat batteries are rarely re-charged to more than 75 per cent of their rated capacity.

The ADVERC (and other) Regulators

Our own battery management has much improved since we fitted the famous ADVERC battery regulator (which used to be the TWC) and was chosen because a lot of work has been done to toughen up its components, which makes them more suitable for the marine environment. It has also been around since 1985 and gained considerable reputation with trucking fleets and marine commercial operators. That is not to say that other regulators are less effective, but on *Abemama* this one has been good news.

The ADVERC and its fellows use a microchip to monitor battery state and to control recharge. It is not a charge accelerator, but works by shutting off the charge current for a milli second in order to view true battery status under unassisted and zero load. Then it regulates the input charge to suit the battery state, that is, cuts it back, or steps it up to a hefty punch without reaching a level where there is so much charge that it bleeds away as wasted heat, or causes gassing. This drop-and-surge technique obviates counter voltage and reduces sulphation sufficiently to give the battery bank a 100 per cent charge.

The system is a very good buy and is easy enough to fit, with push-on clips, or plugs behind the alternator cover and a single wire to the battery and its blocking diode. It comes complete with a by-pass, which passes functionality back to the alternator's own regulator should the electronic version ever fail. It is a very useful piece of gear and leads the way in making boat owners realise that the regulator is probably the most crucial element in any charging system. If you go far off-shore, or get gale-bound in harbour, you ignore it at your peril.

Solution Four: A Generator

Like many yachts we carry a small, two-stroke generator, which was originally acquired with emergency battery charging in mind. Luckily, we have only ever needed to use it in this mode on one occasion and that was a couple of days after we bought the boat and were at our most vulnerable. We do not substitute it for running the main engine for routine recharging because it is noisy, smelly if left in a cockpit locker and less efficient. If you are tempted to use one as a prime recharger, make sure that you can access mains-level voltage and use a battery charger. Restoring battery health from the DC side of a small generator takes forever.

In spite of not having used the generator for its originally intended purpose, I would not like to be at sea without it. On a number of occasions it has been a really useful runner of power tools, a sharpener and used to take over other functions whilst we are doing jobs involving disconnecting the boat's principal supply.

That probably says it all about marine electronics. We buy equipment for one function and find other uses for it as we go along. There is no substitute for experience.

Conclusion

I hope that you have enjoyed reading this book as much as I have enjoyed writing it. Authors are commissioned to write technical books because they know a lot about the subject. It is only when you start on such a wide topic as marine electronics that you realise that there is still plenty to learn. I am still learning.

When you plan the pages, you also wish that you could find enough space to share even more of the experiences and pleasure which working and playing in the electronics field has brought. You also wish that you could have included many more products such as radar reflectors, epirbs, satellite telephones, etc. To paraphrase Toscanini, it is such a shame that there are so many beautiful women in the world and so little time.

There are now many boat owners and boat enthusiasts with whom I have discussed topics similar to the contents of this book's separate chapters. I have enjoyed talking to them all and several of them have become firm cruising and diving friends.

Getting to know them has been a spin-off pleasure from involvement with marine electronics. It brings back to mind the idea in the Introduction that we purchase equipment for boat safety and efficiency, but there should also be a large pinch of pleasure in the recipe.

We only have one life, so let us hope that boat toys can bring some extra pleasure to it.

Index

target height, 60
three dimension sounder, 77
tidal data, 126
tiller pilot, 88
touch pad, 84
transceiver, 9
  stability, 26
transducer, 70, 73, 80
transmit power, 66
type approval, 13, 20

ultra high frequency (UHF), 24

variable range marker, 65
very high frequency (VHF), 9, 24, 39
  radio range, 11

waterproofing, 20
waypoint, 59
weather, 36, 45
weatherfax, 36, 45, 48
wheel pilot, 88
whip, 12
working channel, 16